WITHDRAWN

DEVELOP YOUR ASSERTIVENESS

CREATING SUCCESS

The best-selling series is back and better than ever

MARCH 2013

Because you only have one chance in life to make a good impression.

DEVELOP YOUR ASSERTIVENESS

SUE BISHOP

CREATING SUCCESS

First published in 1996 by Kogan Page Limited
Second edition 2000
Reissued in 2006, 2010
Third edition 2013

2nd Floor, 45 Gee Street	1518 Walnut Street, Suite 1100	4737/23 Ansari Road
London EC1V 3RS	Philadelphia PA 19102	Daryaganj
United Kingdom	USA	New Delhi 110002
www.koganpage.com		India

© Sue Bishop, 1996, 2000, 2006, 2010, 2013

The right of Sue Bishop to be identified as the author of this work has been asserted by her in accordance with the Copyright, Designs and Patents Act 1988.

ISBN   978 0 7494 6698 5
E-ISBN   978 0 7494 6699 2

British Library Cataloguing-in-Publication Data

A CIP record for this book is available from the British Library.

Library of Congress Cataloging-in-Publication Data

Bishop, Sue, 1949-
   Develop your assertiveness / Sue Bishop. – 3rd Edition.
      pages cm
   ISBN 978-0-7494-6698-5 – ISBN (invalid) 978-0-7494-6699-2 (ebk.)
1. Organizational behavior. 2. Assertiveness training. 3. Assertiveness (Psychology)
4. Interpersonal relations. I. Title.
   HD58.7.B565 2013
   650.1′3–dc23   2012045518

Typeset by Graphicraft Limited, Hong Kong
Printed and bound by CPI Group (UK) Ltd, Croydon, CR0 4YY

CONTENTS

INTRODUCTION

So just what is assertiveness? What does being assertive entail? It's about being able to express yourself with confidence without having to resort to passive, aggressive or manipulative behaviour. It involves greater self-awareness; getting to know, like and be in charge of the real 'you'. It requires listening and responding to the needs of others without neglecting your own interests or compromising your principles. It is about improving your interpersonal skills; more effective communication; controlling stress through a better handling of problem people and situations. It is about choice – being able to express your needs, opinions or feelings, confident that you will not be dominated, exploited or coerced against your wishes.

Assertiveness is about effective communication and this does not just mean choosing the right words to say in a given situation. Tone of voice, intonation, volume, facial expression, gesture and body language all play a part in the message you are sending to the other person, and unless all parts of the equation match, you will be sending a garbled message.

Generally, if you are putting yourself or the other person down in some way, your communication style is not assertive. Although there will be times when you choose to be passive, or use more aggressive 'muscle', an assertive response is invariably the preferable one, and leads to win–win situations where both parties feel good about themselves. Assertive skills can be learnt, and later chapters explore the various approaches and techniques that can be applied.

TO BE, OR NOT TO BE?

CONDITIONING

When you first entered this world, and until you were about six months old, you knew and demonstrated two forms of behaviour: passive, dependent behaviour and aggressive, demanding behaviour. As you grew older, one of the first words you will have learnt and uttered is 'No'. This is a way of saying, 'I can now begin to rationalize, to make my own decisions.' It is a way of beginning to establish independence as a unique individual.

For toddlers, being passive sometimes, aggressive at others, freely expressing feelings, and saying 'No' without guilt or malice, is spontaneous and natural. Were you reprimanded for saying 'No' as a small child? Were you told it was not polite... might hurt others' feelings... make you unpopular? Might this have a bearing on why you might find it difficult to utter the 'No' word today?

In our early development we were conditioned by people and events, and soon adapted to please parents or other adults responsible for our social training. We were told what was good and what was bad; what to do and what not to do. It is often in a child's best interests to please or submit – good behaviour is rewarded with smiles and favours. Sometimes bad behaviour gets its rewards as well – *thinks*...'If I can't get her attention any other way, I'll scream, yell and throw things; any attention – even a telling off – is better than being ignored'. You can see how the passive/ aggressive pattern builds and how as adults we slide into adapted behaviour to achieve our own ends, to keep the peace or to meet the needs of others – often to the detriment of our own well-being.

Passive and aggressive behaviours come naturally to us and often seem the easy (though seldom the most effective) option, whereas assertive behaviour requires a cognitive process rather than a gut reaction. It is learnt – we were not born assertive. Depending on our own mood, the situation, the people involved and so on, we frequently respond somewhere along the spectrum of passive-through-aggressive without considering the assertive option which recognizes the needs, feelings and opinions of both you and the other person.

Conditioning plays a large part in the way you act and react as an adult. Role expectations come into this too. We may have mentally ingested that it is unladylike to express anger, or that it is a sign of weakness to cry in public, or that men should be aggressively ambitious, enjoy physical contact sports and so on. Subtle conditioning has coloured the way we see ourselves and others, but the good news is that conditioning has not fixed your personality for ever. You are constantly developing and changing. Things learnt can be unlearnt, alternative behaviours can be rehearsed and practised until they become second nature.

APPROPRIATE BEHAVIOUR CHOICE

Before moving on to look at various aspects of assertiveness training, it should be stressed that passive and aggressive behaviours are not necessarily bad. They can both be appropriate at times – righteous indignation at social injustices, for example. The assertive option might not always be the best behaviour choice. To test how *effective* your present behaviour is, try the following.

EXERCISE

Tick the response which best represents how you would react to each situation, *not* what you consider to be the correct response; then check with the comments below.

1 You work for an organization which has a strong equal opportunities policy. One of your staff has already been warned about racist remarks. You overhear him telling a racist joke to a colleague.

   a 'I've explained why jokes such as these are offensive. It's also company policy not to use sexist or racist language in the workplace. Do you have a problem with this which you would like to discuss?'

   b 'I know you think that racist jokes are just a bit of fun. If it were down to me…but it's the rules you know, and if the boss heard, it would be my neck on the line.'

   c 'You've been told about expressing racist views before. This is your final warning. Disobey company rules again and you're looking at dismissal.'

2 You have had complaints about the offhand manner of one of your staff. You call her into your office to talk about the problem. Before you can open the discussion, tearfully she says, 'I know what this is about, and yes, I have been short-tempered – even rude – to some customers recently,

---

but I am so worried about my husband; he's having tests for a blood disorder.'

a 'That's all very well, but our business is suffering because of your attitude. You'll have to learn to leave your problems at home and give 100 per cent to the company while you're here.'

b 'I'm so sorry; I'd no idea he was ill. Is there any way we can help you – would a chat with the welfare section help...?'

c 'I thought there must be some explanation. I'm sorry that you have problems at home. However, we expect a certain standard from our staff, and complaints have been made which must be followed up.'

3 One of your staff has made a minor error, unnoticed by you, but picked up by your boss who storms into the office and says to you, 'These are the wrong widgets. You're so careless – call yourself a supervisor?'

a 'You're right. I'm really sorry... I should have checked. It won't happen again. I'll get it sorted out right away.'

b 'Who got up on the wrong side of the bed this morning then? I'll ignore your remarks – you're obviously not yourself today!'

c 'I'm sorry that we made a mistake with this order. However, you're wrong to say that I am careless, and I resent your remarks about my supervisory skills. My standards and those of my team are high. Mistakes sometimes happen.'

COMMENTS

1 *Option (a)* is assertive, but this member of staff knows the rules and has already been given a warning. An approach further along the aggressive scale would be more effective.

Option (b) is not only passive, but shows poor management style, colluding with the 'offenders' rather than defending company policy.

Option (c), although blunt to the point of being aggressive, has about the right amount of muscle to be effective, leaving the offender in no doubt as to where he stands.

2 *Option (a)* is not only aggressive, but insensitive and inappropriate in the circumstances.

Option (b), although passive, would be the most appropriate and effective way of dealing with this situation at present.

Option (c) is assertive, but is assertiveness really an appropriate behaviour choice in this situation? A response further along the passive scale is called for.

3 *Option (a)* is far too passive. Forelock tugging when you or your team have been verbally attacked is just asking for future abuse.

Option (b) just *might* be OK if you know your boss really well and can joke him out of his mood. However, it could be taken as rude and aggressive and, more importantly, doesn't address the fact that *you* – not just your work – have been verbally attacked.

Option (c) is both assertive and an appropriate response to the boss's attack. It recognizes and apologizes for a genuine mistake, but doesn't let him get away with unjust criticism of you or your team.

KEY POINTS

- We are not born assertive; early conditioning directs behaviour choice and actions.

- Assertiveness is an effective behaviour choice which can be learnt.

PREPARE TO ASSERT YOURSELF

In the same way that it is impossible to become assertive just by reading a book on the subject – you have to practise assertion skills – it is also impossible to appear assertive with the tensed muscles and pounding heart associated with stress. Your body language will give you away. Whatever words you choose to say, however 'assertive' they might be, if delivered with the wrong tone of voice, too much or too little volume, or accompanied by inappropriate facial expression and posture, your assertiveness will be ineffective. You will be perceived as apprehensive, emotional, hostile or aggressive by the other person.

Let's face it, while most of us would like to be assertive most of the time, the occasions where this proves most difficult are those where it is really important to display assertiveness skills. These are also occasions when we are likely to feel the most tense. Imagine the following scenarios.

EXERCISE

1 You are summoned to the boss's office and can tell by the look on his face that it's not to talk about your next pay rise or promotion!

2 Your parent or an elderly relative expects to spend Christmas with you. You and your partner want a quiet Christmas together. You have just called at her house to tell this relative that you can't have her to stay.

3 You decide now is the time to confront your partner with an issue about which you know there will be some disagreement.

4 Although you've explained the cause for the delay, your client continues to behave in a quarrelsome and aggressive manner.

5 It's down to you to tell a member of staff about a personal hygiene problem.

COMMENTS

You may not have been in any of these precise situations, but you can imagine – even begin to experience – some of the symptoms of anxiety you are likely to display: the dry mouth, the sweating palms, the tightening of the facial muscles, the thumping heart, the churning tummy and, not least, feelings of self-doubt about the outcome of the ensuing interaction.

Even attending an assertiveness training course will be a source of stress for most of us. 'Performing' in a role-play for the first time can be traumatic, however much we might agree with the principle that it is the best way to practise new skills in a safe environment.

TENSION CONTROL

This short chapter will look at what I consider to be an essential precursor to assertiveness training: tension control. However good you become at mastering the theory of assertiveness, if anxiety produces observable signs of your apprehension, this will convey itself to the other person – even at a subconscious level – and communication will suffer as a result.

There are a number of coping strategies. For example, you could have a stiff drink before an important encounter, go into a meditative trance, or practise deep-breathing exercises. However, unless you carry a hip flask, a stiff drink is seldom available just when you need one (and it's bad for your health). Transcendental meditation can be difficult to achieve in a crowded department store, and deep breathing is impossible with stomach muscles in a knot! For these reasons, I suggest you try these alternative methods. The beauty of them is that they can be practised at any time, anywhere, at short notice. They are an unobtrusive and effective way to control nervousness and reduce negative feelings such as anger and stress.

EXERCISE

1 Clench everything you can as tightly as you can: toes and feet, buttocks, leg and arm muscles, fists and, if no one is looking, screw up your face as well. Hold for a second or two, then quickly release all the tension from the muscles. Go as limp as you can or your environment will allow! Repeat it if you can. You should now be able to take one or two deep breaths and be ready to take on the world.

2 This technique was perfected by Dorothy Sarnoff and is explained in detail in her book *Never be Nervous Again*

(1988) Century Hutchinson, London. It involves tensing then relaxing the muscles under the diaphragm. Press the palms of your hands together, fingers pointing upwards, forearms horizontal with the floor. Push until you feel the pressure in the heels of the palms and under your arms. Breathe in, then let the breath out slowly and gently, through a slightly open mouth. While breathing out, tighten the muscles in that triangle between the ribs. Relax the muscles at the end of the exhalation. Breathe in gently. Repeat it if you can.

This exercise has the added advantage of aiding voice control – you will be able to communicate without a nervous tremble in your voice, and project without excessive volume or shouting.

COMMENTS

Don't forget that it's equally important to unwind after coping with a stressful situation. Most people will find that it is time well spent to find a relaxation technique which suits them.

INNER CALM

Be kind to yourself and allow a few minutes each day to relax your body by whatever method you are comfortable with. Listen to calming music; meditate; soak in a hot bath – or do all three simultaneously! When your body is at ease, imagine yourself in a place of beauty and calm, where you feel at peace with the world. For me this would be on the shores of my favourite lake in Cumbria, in the north of England. You might prefer to imagine lying in the hot sun on a golden beach listening to the waves, or enjoying a woodland walk full of spring flowers and birdsong. You might feel happiest at a concert or ballet where you can lose yourself in the colour, images and sounds. Employ your imagination and concentrate on the sensations you are experiencing. What sounds can you hear? What can you see? How do you feel? You are now exercising your mind in a positive way, emptying it of unhelpful distractions, learning to achieve an inner calm and so increasing your ability to function assertively, whatever life deals you.

KEY POINTS

- Difficult situations, creating anxiety or stress, can compromise assertive behaviour.
- Simple relaxation techniques and coping strategies can be learnt.

POSITIVE THINKING

Assertiveness training has been around for a good many years now and has had a chequered press, some seeing it as training in how to get your own way – which it isn't; or how to become as aggressive as the next person – which it also isn't.

Assertiveness training can be of immense benefit as a means of self-development. People with good assertiveness skills will also have enhanced self-awareness, greater confidence and self-esteem, and honest, powerful and effective communication skills. They will have respect for themselves and for others.

Central to all this is positive thinking. Assertive people have a positive self-image; they will use positive language; they will look for positive outcomes to interactions; they will work with the other person to provide positive solutions to problems by which both sides 'win'; they will be positive in their respect for the other person's views and opinions, whether or not they share these views.

Let's look at each of these areas in turn to see how they can be developed.

SELF-AWARENESS AND SELF-ESTEEM

People come to assertiveness training for a number of reasons: to improve their people skills; to help tilt the balance from aggressive communication patterns to a more calm, rational approach; to gain confidence so that they are not so often seen as weak, an 'easy touch', the office or family 'doormat'; to learn to stand up for their rights, and so on.

Having agreed that there are occasions when communication somewhere along the passive or aggressive spectrum is appropriate, and remembering that assertiveness is always a choice of behaviour, you should recognize that if you habitually function in a passive or aggressive way, it can be bad for your health, and certainly won't win you friends or enable you to influence people. A common factor to both aggressive and passive behaviour is low self-esteem.

So how can you begin to like yourself a little more? First, you've got to know yourself – to see yourself, 'warts and all'. To help you to do this, complete the following exercise.

EXERCISE

1 Take a sheet of paper (you may need a large one!) and list all the things you *don't like about yourself*. You can include negative qualities identified by others if you wish – how others see you. Allow yourself at least ten minutes. Be brutally honest – only you have to see the list.

   Now consider each item carefully, and underline any negative quality about which you feel you can do absolutely nothing. For example, you may hate being short, but that's how nature made you, so there's no use fretting over it or bemoaning the fact – it's something you have to live with.

You may have problems in your life over which you have had little control, such as bereavement or illness. These are things you have to accept – and like yourself in spite of them. We will return to how you can begin to do that in a moment.

2 Next, put a tick against any negative quality you are *prepared to accept about yourself*. For example, friends may 'accuse' you of over-reacting to some situations, but you may feel that being highly sensitive to some issues actually motivates you to do something about them. Consider where this is a positive force for you, and stick with it. However, where it is not productive, but a source of anxiety which stifles action or development, you will need to find ways of doing something about this tendency to over-react.

3 Which brings us to the third part of the exercise. Circle all the faults, failings and negative behaviour traits which *you would like to change*. You know you have a 'short fuse', for example, and can explode with anger, hurting yourself and others in the process; or you find it difficult to give or take criticism. There are assertiveness techniques, described later, which can help with these issues. Keep your list, and when you have finished reading the book, see how the techniques can begin to help you overcome these negative traits.

Before moving on, let's take another look at the first area: faults and failings, things you don't like about yourself, about which you can do nothing. Is this really the case? Do you just have to accept your lot? You *may* have to, but can you turn any of these areas into a positive experience?

Look again at the items you've underlined. What good has come out of them? Can you see, in any of them, areas for development and growth? For instance, if 'getting old' is one of the things you don't like about yourself – and let's face it, the ageing process is inevitable; it happens to us all and few of us enjoy it – then what can you list that's positive about it? Go on, forget your negativity for once – the wrinkles and lines and the constant battle to defy gravity and keep your body in shape. Accept, and look for the good things.

A friend of mine, chronically ill, has been unable to work for several years now and has to rely on state benefit and meagre savings. Fact – she's in pain much of the time; fact – she's short of money; fact – she resents taking and not giving; fact – she could get depressed at her lot. She could become one of the moan-and-groan brigade and feel justified in saying that there is nothing positive she can do about her situation. However, she keeps her self-esteem (and her friends) by giving what she *has* got which is her time, her care, her talents, her ability to listen, her cheerfulness and her friendship – which is invaluable.

Keep reviewing your list, looking for the positive, the possibilities, the challenges. Be active in your pursuit of a positive self-image.

POSITIVE SELF-IMAGE

Have you ever felt you were wearing the wrong clothes at a party? Or have you realized, too late, that there is a coffee stain down the front of your blouse/shirt while attending an important meeting? Things like this knock your confidence because you are aware that you are not presenting the best image to other people. Undermined confidence equals a lowering of self-esteem which can in turn produce non-assertive behaviour.

The image you present to others, whether by your physical appearance, the clothes or hairstyle you choose or the body language you use, has a lot to do with whether or not they perceive you as assertive. You can choose all the right words and deliver them with the correct emphasis and volume, but if your body language doesn't match your verbal communication, the message you are sending will be garbled. The receiver will take more notice of what is seen than what is heard – a hard truth, but a statistically proven fact.

EXERCISE

Sit in front of a mirror and imagine yourself in the following situations. Really get into the spirit of things! Note how your facial expressions, gestures, the way you hold your body and so on, subtly change.

1 You are sitting in a traffic jam. No one is going anywhere, but the man in the car behind you incessantly blows his horn.

2 Your boss is giving you a real dressing down for something you know you haven't done. You are arguing your corner when suddenly it dawns on you that he is right and that you've made a dreadful gaffe.

3 You are smartly dressed in readiness for an important interview. Walking along the street, you are deliberately splashed with muddy water by a youth on a bike, who instead of riding off, turns with a grin on his face to confront you.

COMMENTS

Things like clenched fists, arms folded tightly across the chest, or standing with hands on hips and a jutting stance are as much a give-away to your angry feelings as are the clenched jaw, frown and fixed gaze which accompany aggressive feelings and behaviour. Anxiety or embarrassment can produce nervous mannerisms, a downcast gaze with a reluctance to look the other person in the eye, and so on.

However, assertive body language reflects a person at ease with him/herself: an open stance, relaxed posture, arms held loosely at sides or resting in lap. There should be no apparent tension in the face muscles, and you should maintain regular eye contact with the other person, neither staring nor averting your gaze.

NB Understanding and improving your non-verbal communication skills is a typical instance where rehearsing with colleagues, getting feedback from others, using closed circuit TV, etc is so beneficial. I do urge you to attend an assertiveness course.

POSITIVE LANGUAGE

Clear, concise, constructive vocabulary is an all-important aspect of assertiveness. So is the ability to phrase things in a positive rather than negative way; it will help your cause, and make the other person feel less threatened and more responsive. For instance, there is a subtle difference between saying to a child 'Don't play with that in here' and 'Would you play with that outside, please', or 'Why can't you clear up after you?' and 'Would you put the cat food away once you've fed him, please'.

Positive phrasing helps to keep conversation on an adult–adult basis and minimizes the risk of it escalating into an argument. Positive thinking also requires positive language to translate 'if only's' into positive action.

EXERCISE

Consider the following 'self-talk' phrases which are neither positive nor assertive. Rewrite them as positive assertions.

Thinks...

1 I really should get down to some studying today.

2 If only I hadn't lost my temper with John today...

3 I can't go to the party; I've much too much to do.

4 Why did I agree to give that presentation? I'll be hopeless.

COMMENTS

Most of us spend far too much time making excuses to ourselves about why we aren't assertive, thinking things like, 'When I feel more in control, I'll speak to him about it' or 'I would discuss it with her, but she'll only get upset'. We also set up a lot of doom and gloom barriers to assertion; thoughts like, 'What if she rejects me?' or 'If I tell them how I feel, they might not ask me again'. With practice, this kind of negative self-talk can be replaced by positive alternatives. Let's look at the few examples above.

1 *Should* in this context is a guilt-ridden word. You can flog yourself to death with 'shoulds'. The implication here could be 'I ought to study but I don't want to'. This sort of indecision and procrastination only causes stress. There is a choice – to study or not to study. Far better positively to assert 'I could study today, but I'm choosing to relax and watch a video', or 'Deadlines are looming so I will concentrate on study today'. Decision made, end of stress.

 Alternatively, this statement could be the response to a request to do something, or go somewhere. As such it is a rather feeble excuse just asking to be shot down in flames. The other person is likely to continue to persuade and coerce. An assertive person would consider the request and either think 'I would like to agree, so I will say "Yes" and study some other time' or say 'My studies must take priority, so no, I won't...'.

2 Self-pity and whining will get you nowhere. What was done or said is history. You were responsible for your loss of control and the results of that. Learn from the experience and make a positive assertion – 'Today I learnt – so next time I'll...'.

3 With a few factual exceptions such as 'I can't eat shellfish – it would make me ill' or 'I can't swim', eliminate *can'ts* from your thoughts. You either will or you won't do something. *Can't* implies 'I would if I could, but...' and opens you up to a barrage of reasons why you *could* if you really wanted to! Make your decision and assertively stick to it, eg 'I'd love to come to the party, but I've a report that I must finish tonight so no, I won't be there.'

Can't is also a word of self-doubt, implying that you have no control over your life. The more times you tell yourself you can't, the lower your self-esteem will become. Remember, assertiveness is about choice. Either you can and you will, or you choose not to. *Can't* doesn't come into it!

4 Statements like 'I'll be hopeless' can easily become self-fulfilling prophecy. Like *can'ts*, such thoughts should be replaced by positive assertions. You did agree to give the presentation so look on it not as a problem, but an opportunity. Don't *hope* it will be OK; *know* that you will manage it well. Think positively, practise using positive language, and you can handle anything.

POSITIVE AFFIRMATIONS

Negative self-talk leads to self-doubt and low self-esteem, yet most of us indulge in a lot of negative inner dialogue – you know the sort of thing:

Thinks…

- 'I've always been useless with anything mechanical.'
- 'I'll never get that finished on time.'
- 'If he does that again I'll explode!'
- 'She must think I'm so stupid.'
- 'I can't cope.'
- 'Perhaps I just don't have what it takes.'
- 'I wish Adam wasn't going to be there. He always makes me feel so inferior.'

Does this kind of thinking make you happy? Does it increase your confidence? Does it increase your effectiveness? Of course not. Miserable thoughts drain you of energy and power. Because the level of assertiveness you are able to generate depends largely on your state of mind – your self-esteem and confidence – it is important to recognize this negative internal chattering and replace it with positive self-talk. Remember the truism of self-fulfilling prophecy. We create our own reality, so it's far better if that reality can be optimistic and positive.

Sadly it is far easier to be negative than positive in our thinking, and one study even suggests that the average adult engages in negative self-talk for as much as 80 per cent of the time! Learning to change a negative into a positive mental attitude will take time and constant practice because a lot of our self-doubt stems from early conditioning and we have probably been telling ourselves – and reinforcing – the same negative messages for years. However, you can retrain your brain to think positively.

So what can you do to bring about this change? First you must recognize negativity in your inner dialogue and when it occurs replace it with a positive, energising, self-elevating pep talk. This may sound simplistic, but it works. You need to state your alternative self-affirmation *out loud* several times. For some reason actually saying the words aloud, perhaps while looking in a mirror, helps you to internalize the positive belief, so instead of listening and believing your inner voice that tells you 'I can't cope', replace this with something like 'Whatever happens, I can handle it'. To give an example, if you are having doubts about entering that half-marathon and feel you will never be able to stay the course, write pep talk messages to yourself and pin them where you can see them – on the fridge, beside your word processor, next to the television, etc. Messages such as:

- 'Every day I'm getting stronger.'
- 'There is nothing to fear.'
- 'I will compete and do myself justice.'
- 'I'm up to this.'

Whenever possible, repeat this – like a mantra – several times, out loud. Surprisingly, it doesn't even matter if your conscious self believes the words. By saying them aloud your inner self will react to this drip, drip process and you will become stronger and more confident.

EXERCISE

Listen to your own inner voice – the one that keeps feeding you negative thoughts. Write down five or six and prioritize them. Which negative self-talk most impairs your confidence or effectiveness? Working on one or two to start with, rewrite these negative thoughts into positive affirmations as suggested above. Ensure that they are written in the present – not happening tomorrow or in the future, but now – eg:

- 'I am a useful member of the team.'
- 'I analyze and learn from my mistakes.'

- 'I do not allow comparisons with others to affect my self-esteem.'
- 'I'm not a failure if I don't succeed. I'm a success because I tried.'

Now do one (or both) of two things. Write your positive affirmations on to postcards and/or repeat them on to an audio recorder. Place the postcards where you will be able to see them several times a day or carry them around in your pocket or bag so that you can refer to them at will. Speak your affirmations – out loud – several times.

COMMENTS

It is important that you hear yourself say them. You are beginning to retrain your brain to think positively. If you speak your affirmations on to an audio tape, make this your bedtime listening, or when you awake in the morning, switch off your alarm clock and tune into your personal pep talk. Have faith. It will work!

POSITIVE OUTCOMES

If an interpersonal conflict threatens, do you avoid confrontation? Do you adopt an 'anything for a quiet life' attitude? Do you set out to 'win' at any price? Do you look for a compromise? Do you try to achieve a win–win solution? Imagine the following scene.

EXERCISE

You and your partner share a car. This is because you normally use a company car, but today it is at the garage for repairs. You have agreed to pick up a colleague to go to an evening meeting and have assumed that you will use your shared car. On arriving home, your partner says that she has arranged to go out for a drink with a non-driving friend, and needs the car to get to the club.

Suggest solutions to the situation against the areas listed above:

1 Avoidance

2 Win–lose

3 Compromise

4 Win–win

COMMENTS

1 You could just give in, suppressing your own needs, if you fear the consequences of a confrontation. By implication, your partner will have 'won', but lowered self-esteem and resentment towards the other person may result.

2 You could sulk until you get your own way, or argue that your need is greater than hers, or simply insist that you take the car. There will always be a winner and a loser in such exchanges, and invariably the relationship will suffer as a result.

3 You could suggest that you take the car to the meeting, but will pay for a cab for your partner and friend, provided you can then have the shared car until your company car is repaired. Compromise may seem a favourable option. Sometimes it is

the best solution possible. However, if both sides give a little in order to gain *something*, often the *best* solution is not achieved – rather a watered-down version of the ideal. At worst, both of you may feel cheated and dissatisfied with the outcome.

4 You could suggest a solution where both of you 'win', neither is inconvenienced or has to expend time, energy or money. Why not drop off your partner and friend at the club before going to the meeting and collect them when your business is finished? In this way, your partner and friend will both be able to drink, and (in this hypothetical situation) you could join them after the meeting. You've also saved the price of a taxi.

A win–win solution is not always possible, but should always be sought by proceeding as follows:

- Think positive; this is a problem-solving exercise not an interpersonal conflict.
- Think of the other person as a partner in problem solving, not an opponent.
- Find out exactly what the other person needs; what they want to gain from the situation, how strong their feelings are about it, and so on.
- Compare this with your own needs, wants, feelings and expectations.
- Establish where there are similarities, differences or where needs might dovetail.
- Look at the options, discuss and evaluate.
- Co-operate; work together towards a win–win solution.
- Always recognize the other person's basic rights while not neglecting your own.

KEY POINTS

- Honest self-appraisal leads to enhanced self-awareness.
- Negative self-talk leads to self-doubt and low self-esteem; you can learn to use self-affirming alternatives.
- Positive thinking is essential to assertive behaviour.
- Assertive people have a positive self-image; will use positive language; look for positive outcomes to interactions; will work with the other person to provide positive solutions by which both sides 'win'.

RIGHTS AND WRONGS

This last point brings us neatly to another important element in assertiveness training: *recognizing your, and the other person's, basic rights*. Most books on assertiveness training will list personal rights, with some variations according to author interpretation. These rights are neither written in tablets of stone nor enforceable by law, but are a common-sense set of rules to aid self-development and enhance interpersonal relationships.

The important point to remember is that for every right you have, the other person has similar rights. For example, you have the right to ask for what you want. The other person has an equal right to refuse your request, or indeed to request something of you. If you ignore or ride roughshod over another's rights, this is aggressive behaviour. If you ignore your own rights, you are being non-assertive and passive. An assertive system of 'rights' has to incorporate mutual respect for each other's needs, opinions and feelings.

The right, from which all your other personal rights is derived, can be stated quite simply:

You have the right to be the final authority for what you are, and what you do.

This is irrespective of the roles you have in life, what others expect of you, or how you feel you *should* behave. This right applies in every area of your life: business, social and personal. Simple to state; easy to agree that you have the right to state your own needs and set your own priorities, to be ultimately responsible for every aspect of your life, but perhaps not too easy to put into practice. Give some thought to what this means; it is a complex philosophy to accept for yourself. It is equally difficult to accept this right in others.

Although there are some basic human rights which appear in all literature on assertiveness, there are almost as many variations on the theme as there are books on the subject. Below you will see listed 40 basic rights, some of which may seem similar, but all of which carry different implications. It would be useful to share your views about the following exercise with a friend or colleague. It will help to identify the subtle differences mentioned and help you to ascertain the relevance of each to your own situation.

EVERYONE'S BASIC RIGHTS

EXERCISE

Consider the rights listed below, compiled from the views of several authors. Think about each in turn; put a mark against those which you have personal difficulty in accepting for yourself. Think, too, about context. For example, you may find it easy to ask for what you want in most circumstances – of your boss, subordinates and friends – but have difficulty in requesting what you *really* want from your partner, parents or children. Or it could be that you find change threatening rather than challenging. Although it is everyone's *right* to change and develop, there are either elements of your personality which are holding you back – or you are allowing others to stunt your personal growth.

Basic rights

1 To be treated as an equal, regardless of gender, race, age or disability.
2 To be treated with respect as a capable human being.
3 To decide how to spend my time.
4 To ask for what I want.
5 To ask for feedback on things such as my performance, behaviour, image.
6 To be listened to and taken seriously.
7 To have an opinion.
8 To hold political beliefs.
9 To cry.
10 To make mistakes.
11 To say 'No' without feeling guilty.
12 To state my needs.
13 To set my own priorities.
14 To express my feelings.
15 To say 'Yes' for myself without feeling selfish.
16 To change my mind.
17 To fail occasionally.
18 To say 'I don't understand'.
19 To make statements with no logical basis and which I do not have to justify.

20 To ask for information.

21 To be successful.

22 To express my beliefs.

23 To adhere to my own set of values.

24 To take time to make decisions.

25 To take responsibility for my own decisions.

26 To have privacy.

27 To admit 'I don't know'.

28 To change/develop as a human being.

29 To choose whether or not to get involved in other people's problems.

30 To decline to be responsible for someone else's problems.

31 To look after my own needs.

32 To have time and space to be alone.

33 To be an individual.

34 To ask for information from professionals.

35 Not to be dependent on others' approval.

36 To be the judge of my own worth.

37 To choose how to behave/respond in a given situation.

38 To be independent.

39 To be me; not the person others want me to be.

40 Not to assert myself.

Hopefully, you are beginning to see areas where you are not asserting your rights or where you are being manipulated or held back from doing so by others. Admittedly, this is a long and soul-searching activity, but an invaluable aid to establishing where you need to concentrate your assertiveness skills.

Identifying personal rights with which you have difficulty is only one half of the equation. Remember that the other person has similar rights. Look at the list again. Which rights do you violate in other people? How do you manipulate others to get your own way?

As a boss, for example, do you ever make a subordinate feel inadequate for saying 'I don't understand' or for asking for information which is second nature to you? Do you allow your partner space and freedom to develop as an individual? Do you *expect* certain things of people because of their role in your life? Do you allow others the right to refuse a request without hectoring them for excuses or asking for justification for their refusal?

Remember that there are two sides to being assertive: respecting the other person's rights while not neglecting your own.

KEY POINTS

- There are two sides to assertive communication. For every right you have, the other person has exactly similar rights.

- Assertive people will be positive in their respect for the other's views and opinions, whether or not they share those views.

- Who you are, what you say, how you act and what you do is ultimately your decision.

NOW AND THEN

HOW ASSERTIVE ARE YOU?

I'm making a rather obvious assumption that you are reading this book either because you feel you would gain from modifying your behaviour in some way, or that you want to improve your interpersonal skills through assertiveness training. It follows, therefore, that at present there are areas in your life where you are not as assertive as you would like to be.

We have established that assertiveness is a *choice* of behaviour and that there are occasions when it is appropriate *not* to assert yourself. We have examined basic rights, and from this you will have deduced areas for self-development. In order to devise your own personal programme for self-improvement, you also need to consider areas of your life where, at present, you find it difficult to assert yourself.

For example, it may be that you always react badly to criticism – getting defensive or aggressive or counter-attacking. It could be that you always feel upset or hurt by criticism and spend endless hours fretting over comments made by others. Or, more likely, it will depend on the particular situation, the person who is criticizing you and your relationship with them, your current mood, state of health, and so on. The following exercise asks you to consider how assertive you feel you are – right now – in certain situations. From this you should be able to devise your own training programme – areas where you need to gain self-confidence and improve your assertiveness skills.

EXERCISE

How assertive are you in the following situations? Do you:

a avoid or repress?

b find being assertive difficult most of the time?

c find it difficult on occasion?

d find it easy to be assertive?

It is unlikely that you will have had exact experience of the scenarios listed, but no doubt you will be able to recall similar situations in your own life.

How do you respond when:

At work

you have to give an honest appraisal which involves negative feedback;

you have to discipline a subordinate for lateness;

there is a personality clash between you and a colleague; she or he always manages to make you extremely angry;

your boss criticizes you (a) justly (b) unjustly;

you have to talk to a subordinate about a sensitive issue, such as making sexual or racial innuendoes;

one of your subordinates has a personal hygiene problem; other members of your team have asked you to say something to her/him;

your boss asks you to do something which you would prefer not to do – such as give a presentation;

you are hurt by a rumour that has been circulated about you;

you need to talk to your boss about better pay or conditions for (a) yourself (b) your staff;

General

your friends are discussing a subject about which you have strong personal views which are contrary to theirs;

the person sitting in front of you at the theatre sits forward in his chair, obliterating your view of the stage;

you have to return some faulty merchandise to a crowded department store;

your car is still stalling a lot though you have returned it twice to the same garage for repair;

professionals hide behind 'technical jargon' when you try to pin them down to a straightforward answer to your questions;

after examination, your doctor fails to explain what he considers to be wrong with you – just silently reaches for his prescription pad;

you are really angry with someone who you feel has taken advantage of your friendship;

a friend has been verbally abused and is too frightened to confront her 'attacker';

At home

you need to say 'No' to the proposed visit of a relative;

constant sniping by a partner, parent or child is threatening your self-worth;

your sexual needs are not matched by your partner's;

you are infuriated by a persistent habit in someone you love;

your partner/parent insists on making decisions for you;

your partner/parent is too dependent on you.

COMMENTS

There are just over 20 situations listed here – no doubt you could think of dozens more, or variations on the themes. It is often difficult to recognize areas of your life where you are being too passive or where you are likely to over-react. Hopefully, by carefully thinking through this exercise, you will begin to see a pattern emerging: where you are too passive and with which people in your life; which situations hit you on the raw, causing hurt or anger; where you repress your feelings rather than assertively tackle problem areas in your life, and so on.

Draw up your own list of situations where you would like to be more assertive. Prioritize them. One word of warning though. Tackle small issues first (where if things should go wrong, it matters little) until you are practised and confident with your assertive skills. Don't think that just by reading books on the subject you are equipped to take on the world and his wife!

KEY POINTS

- Be aware of where you are currently on the passive–through–aggressive spectrum.
- Identify areas you need to develop in a more positive way.

NOW SEE HEAR

LISTENING

There is no point in talking, however assertively, if no one is listening and, conversely, no point in listening if we are not truly attentive to the other person, analyzing the content of their communication and assessing how their tone of voice, mannerisms, facial expressions and so on, add meaning to the words they use.

Think back to everyone's basic rights discussed in Chapter 4. How can you show respect for another person if you do not give them your full attention – actively listen to them – hearing them out rather than impatiently waiting for your turn to talk. Don't you expect the same of others – to be listened to and taken seriously? Yet I'm sure you'll agree that few people have good listening skills. It's all too easy to switch off and become distracted by our own concerns or thoughts about what we're going to do or say next.

One reason for including a chapter on listening here is because of concerns expressed by people attending assertiveness courses, many of whom are helped by improved listening skills. For example, non-assertive people who are shy or lacking in confidence often find it difficult to begin conversations with others, especially on social occasions where they feel they have no aptitude for small talk.

Many people find it relatively easy to communicate on a professional level, when the content of conversation is technical, technological or business orientated, but flounder when they have to step from behind their proverbial desks and chat with superiors, co-workers, clients and customers on a more personal level. On training courses participants previously unknown to each other will soon talk together about work-related issues – common objectives – but some flounder during refreshment breaks where social chit-chat is required.

Concentrating on the other person – finding out about their experiences, beliefs and attitudes – is the way forward. Active listening can really help you tune into the other person and establish a basis for solid communication.

At the other end of the spectrum are the 'short fuse brigade', who find that too often differences of opinion escalate into aggressive outbursts. If this is your tendency, you too will benefit from paying more attention to the other person. Here too, listening is of paramount importance.

Then there are the non-assertive individuals whose self-confidence plummets when others don't listen to them. Well, admit it, haven't you ever been made to feel inadequate or boring when another cuts you short in order to express their own views, or changes the subject before you've finished speaking? How do you cope with people who continually interrupt, or whose topic-hopping makes it virtually impossible for you to maintain a dialogue? How do you stop your boss when he's in full flow, to explain that you are unsure of something he has said, before he disappears for his next meeting believing that he's been heard and fully understood?

These are just some of the issues which need to be addressed by improving your own listening skills and helping others to pay you the attention you deserve.

First, let's examine the plight of the person with a communication block because of a lack of social assertiveness.

THE ART OF SMALL TALK

Rule number one: far better to be a good listener than a person who talks a lot but has nothing to say! Second rule: by watching carefully, listening attentively and questioning skilfully, your attention will be drawn away from your self-consciousness. The other person will be prompted to do most of the talking – at least until you feel more relaxed, confident and able to participate fully in a dialogue.

If the person with whom you wish to start a conversation is unknown to you, you could always begin with a non-threatening statement to 'test the water' – something like, 'There are more people here than I expected.' The other's response and general attitude will show whether they wish to open communication with you. If you are given the green light, continue by asking questions to establish common ground. Let me give you an example.

Anxious party-goer: I work with Mike. Are you a friend of his?

Stranger: Yes, we play badminton together.

Still anxious party-goer: That's interesting; I used to play a lot. Which courts do you use?

Now casual acquaintance: The ones at the Pickstaff Leisure Centre at Bratford.

More relaxed party-goer: What do you think of the Leisure Centre?

Acquaintance: I think it's gone downhill since the latest takeover. We used to be able to book courts a week in advance, have a drink afterwards – a good evening out.

Relaxed party-goer: What's it like now then?

Potential new friend: Well, take what happened last week. We had our game as usual and then...

If only it were as easy as that, I hear you cry! Well it can be. Generally, people like to talk about themselves and their experiences. Listen attentively and you will realize that they also offer free information on which you can build.

In the above example, early on the acquaintance revealed that he played badminton. Now a person who talks rather than listens could have gone on to bore the new acquaintance with his own experiences of playing the game. Instead he chose to offer some free information of his own – 'I used to play a lot' – which provides the acquaintance with an opening later if he chooses to follow it up. He then goes on to ask, 'Which courts do you use?' which shows an interest and invites the acquaintance to give more detail. His next question, 'What do you think of the Leisure Centre?' further opens up the communication process. Note that he asks 'What do *you* think...' rather than 'What's the Leisure Centre like?' The latter would tell him about the Leisure Centre; the former gives information about the acquaintance's views, opinions, feelings, etc. Thus, relationships are built, not by lengthy self-disclosure, but listening attentively and showing a genuine interest in the other person.

Obviously, there are dozens of ways to continue any conversation, but one example for the second dialogue would be to ask something like, 'What is it about evening meetings that tires you?' rather than a closed question such as, 'You prefer day-time meetings then?' or a conversation stopper such as 'So do I.'

The last example above could continue by asking A why she chose to go to St Lucia, or what she thought of the island, both of which help to show A that it's her views, preferences and opinions that are interesting.

The secret of good small-talk technique is to have the courage to make the first move – ask an appropriate question in a friendly and open manner – then listen attentively to the other person's responses. Without interrogating or prying, concentrate on their self-interest and pick up the clues from the free information they give you. Focus on their point of view. Go on to look for areas of common interest.

Being able to engage in small talk is useful, not just for socializing or meeting new friends, but in all sorts of work situations. If you are holding a selection interview, it helps put interviewees at their ease. You can begin to familiarize yourself with each other's vocabulary, style of speaking and personality. A few minutes' small talk helps create a suitable environment for appraisal interviews.

At meetings, a period of social interaction before getting down to business can encourage a relaxed atmosphere and establish team spirit. It can be used to ensure that everyone is involved from the outset, allowing quieter members to contribute early in a non-threatening way. Not least, it can be put to good use to show the other person that you are interested in them as a person, not just as a co-worker.

CONFLICT RESOLUTION

If shyness is not your problem, rather a tendency to be a bit too outspoken when differences of opinion arise, here too improved

EXERCISE

Suggest appropriate follow-up questions in the dialogues below:

a 'No, I didn't drive here; I came by train.'

b _____

_____

a 'No, actually; I find these evening meetings quite exhausting.'

b _____

_____

a 'Yes, I have got a good sun tan. We've just come back from St Lucia.'

b _____

_____

COMMENTS

The trick is to ask open questions – that is, ones which can't be answered by just 'Yes' or 'No'. This prompts the other person to give more information on which you can build a conversation. If B's follow-up question to the first dialogue was 'Do you prefer to travel by train?' A could just give a Yes or No response. Far better to ask 'Why did you choose to travel by train?' which encourages A to explain why he left his car, his views about travel comfort, his opinion on drinking and driving, etc. In other words, it gives A scope to talk and you to listen for more free information on which you can build a dialogue.

listening skills can help. Rather than *react*, jump in and aggressively attack the other person's viewpoint while defending your own, try to be *proactive*.

Engage the other person in conversation to establish their point of view. Question calmly; listen – *really listen* – to what they feel, need or want. Where and how do these differ from your feelings, needs or wants? Express these clearly and rationally. Are there valid points in the other's argument that you can acknowledge? Is there common ground? Are there areas where your views dovetail? Even if the only similarity between you is the force with which you hold your personal views, this can often be expressed to some effect! What are the options for reaching an amicable solution? Do you need to agree to disagree?

If it is obvious that you are really listening to the other person – hearing, understanding and empathizing with their point of view (even if you don't agree with it) – conflict can be resolved, or at least contained, in an adult manner, with the minimum of stress to both parties.

'Nothing is quite so annoying as to have someone go right on talking when you're interrupting.' (Author unknown)

So what can we do to make others better listeners; to encourage them to let us have our say before butting in? First, let's look at some of the reasons we all switch off and stop listening. There will be some factors common to everyone, not least the need to gather our own thoughts before responding in a conversation. Our physical well-being – or lack of it – can influence how well we actively listen. For example, a pang of hunger will immediately turn our attention away from what the other person is saying to thoughts of chocolate bars or how close it is to lunch break.

There are other factors that are individual to you, and may well change at different times and in different situations. To give you a personal example: my first reaction is to switch off the moment a member of a group to which I belong enters the room. I know that she will make a beeline for me and tell the same long-winded story I've heard countless times before. I know that this is a problem for me, and that I have to make a conscious effort to listen carefully, to pay full attention, to ask pertinent questions, to move the dialogue along using my assertiveness skills to respond to her needs while not neglecting my own.

EXERCISE

List in the space below reasons why you, personally, might switch off and stop listening. Think of situations, such as meetings, social gatherings, attending school functions or church ceremonies. Consider individuals you know and what makes it difficult to maintain active listening with some. Why do you sometimes switch off when your partner is talking to you? Are you as alert when listening to your subordinates as with people in authority? What are the barriers? Remember occasions when you've been caught out – what started you day-dreaming?

_____

_____

_____

_____

_____

_____

_____

_____

_____

_____

COMMENTS

We all need to recognize where to cultivate our listening skills, both generally and specifically. As with other areas of assertiveness training, honest self-appraisal leading to enhanced self-awareness is fundamental to improving skills.

Effective listening takes practice, commitment and energy; it's not a passive process. Here are a few tips on improving listening skills.

- Concentrate more on the other person. Read the signs: how do body language, speech patterns and rhythms, levels of apparent tension or calmness add to the meaning of what she's saying?

- Acknowledge to yourself, then consciously block out, barriers to listening such as what you *feel* about the speaker (eg don't like her style of dress, accent, tone of voice etc). Don't be distracted by exterior 'noise'.

- Use spare thinking capacity to summarize and review, and to anticipate where the speaker is leading (but keep tight reins on this or you will be 'tuned out' for too long!).

- Sift information, sorting facts from assumptions, and hard evidence from views and opinions.

- On a one-to-one basis, be involved in the conversation. Encourage the speaker by your attentiveness, expressions of interest and by asking questions. Read between the lines for non-verbal, hidden meanings.

You can practise listening skills, in a practical way, by listening attentively to newscasters or to factual documentary programmes on TV or radio. Use an audio- or videotape to record about ten minutes of talking. See how much you can remember: (a) of essential information; (b) of actual words and phrases used; (c) about the speaker – speech patterns, body language and so on.

Finally, how assertively to stop a person from interrupting, changing the subject or not listening because of a preoccupation with self-interest. Sorry, but there's not a foolproof simple answer to this one. The important point is to keep your cool. Show by your attitude that you want to share in a meaningful dialogue, smile or keep an open expression, and be persistent in your expectation of equal air space. Here are a few tactful interjections you could try.

> 'That's interesting; could I say something here...'; or
>
> 'Before we talk about... there's something you said earlier that I feel very strongly about and would like your views on'; or
>
> 'I'd like to make a point here...'.

Use appropriate body language to let the other person know you intend to assert your right fully to participate in the conversation. Maintain good eye contact. If necessary, you may have to interrupt the other's flow. Do this by getting their attention (eye contact again) using their name and (if, *and only if*, you are both comfortable with physical contact) a hand lightly on the arm.

> 'Sheila, we're both so eager to make a point I feel that neither of us is really listening to the other. There's something you mentioned earlier that I'd like to comment on...
>
> ... What do you think?'

In this way you are acknowledging that neither of you is listening as well as you might, and you are encouraging a two-way flow of conversation.

KEY POINTS

- Active listening involves full attention to the complete message the other person is sending – by their choice of words, tone of voice, body language and non-verbal cues.

- Learn the art of small talk by concentrating primarily on the other person.

- In conflict resolution, learn how to be assertively proactive rather than reactive.

- Use assertiveness skills to claim equal air-space in a conversation.

BODY TALK

We touched on the subject of body language and non-verbal communication in Chapter 3 when we looked at developing a positive self-image. I'd like to look more closely at this fascinating subject before moving on to verbal communication techniques.

BODY LANGUAGE

We've just discussed the importance of listening in the communication process, and maintaining good eye contact was mentioned. You will find that with practice it is relatively easy to look the other person in the eye while you are listening. However, the *manner* in which you look is important.

An acquaintance of mine has a magnificent smile. It lights up her face and makes you feel truly rewarded – when you can make it happen! As you speak to her she fixes you with a concentrated frown (better described as a scowl) and neither blinks nor shows any reaction in her face to what you are saying.

I recently found out that she has a hearing impairment, and her unblinking scowl is really an expression of intense concentration as she attempts to lip read. Her eventual beaming smile is a recognition that she has understood and is able then to engage in meaningful conversation.

I give this example to illustrate how a concentrated face can often look forbidding, so beware. Keep an attentive, responsive expression on your face, ensuring that your expression is compatible with what is being expressed. You will need to break eye contact from time to time, because staring can be very intimidating and seen as an aggressive mode of behaviour, but most of the time you are listening, keep your gaze within the imaginary triangle produced by the brows and nose.

While listening, the occasional 'uh huh' or 'I see' acts as encouragement for the speaker to continue and give more detail. While not literally non-verbal, these are noises of affirmation rather than contributions to conversation. Nods of the head also act as affirmation that you are still with the speaker and it's OK for him or her to continue. Your body language – how you are sitting in the chair, forward and interested, or slumped and bored – is a good indicator of how the speaker's words are being received, as is what you are doing with your hands in relation to your face. Think about this for a moment.

EXERCISE

How might you use your hands, in relation to your face, to indicate the following emotions to the other person:

1 real interest
2 scepticism
3 boredom
4 confusion.

COMMENTS

There are many variations on a theme here, and I wouldn't suggest for one moment that you study the subject of body language in order to manipulate situations to your advantage. However, here are some suggestions regarding how you might have used your hands to indicate the above emotions.

1 hands steepled against lips with possible accompanying concentrated expression and nodding of head;
2 forefinger above lips with rest of hand cradling chin; or tugging an ear lobe;
3 chin resting in fisted hand;
4 rubbing of forehead.

(**NB** No single gesture or movement can give the impression of self-assured confidence, for example. Gestures occur in clusters and are interpreted as a whole.)

If you physically tried the four poses suggested above you will have noticed how your body language can actually dictate your mood. Adopt a bored pose and you will soon feel bored. Curl in on yourself, sigh a few times, bite on your knuckles, and you will soon feel your mood lower and tension setting in.

This works both ways; you can make body language work for you. For example, if you dress well in clothes that you know suit you and that are appropriate to the occasion, and adopt an upright, open, confident pose, I'll guarantee that you'll be far better equipped to take on the world than if you slouch along in tired-looking clothes. Even if you feel low, smile at other people, to yourself in the mirror even, and your mood will begin to lift. It's really true; you can con your subconscious into believing and reacting to any mood you choose.

Let's return to body language and the communication process. In conversation, when it's your turn to speak you will find it much more difficult to maintain eye contact. This is because we need to look away occasionally, at something neutral, in order to focus our thoughts and select appropriate vocabulary to communicate meaning in the best possible way.

This does not mean that we can neglect eye contact, however. It is important to maintain regular eye contact with the listener for a number of reasons. It increases the impact of our communication: if the message is important, increase eye contact. Looking regularly at the listener helps their concentration and makes them feel bonded within the conversation.

Most importantly, eye contact helps you check on how your words are affecting the listener. Obviously, your interpretation will depend on your knowledge of the other person, and the situation. You need reassurance that there is understanding, and the first clue to this is in the other person's facial expression and gesture.

For example, a slight frown could mean that they are confused or have not fully understood you, or that there is an area of disagreement that needs clearing up before you continue. It could just mean that they are concentrating hard on what you're saying, but again, this needs to be checked out before you proceed. A frown accompanied by a grimace could indicate that you've waxed lyrical for too long, and that it's their turn to contribute and, of course, a yawn says it all! Practise reading the signs.

To communicate effectively, words, delivery and body language must be compatible. If everything matches and is consistent, meaning is reinforced. Often though, through nervousness, embarrassment, poorly concealed anger or annoyance we give out conflicting messages, where what we say is contradicted by our facial expression, movement or how we hold our bodies. Body language gives us away.

Unfortunately, in any interaction we don't first consciously think about words and meaning; we *feel* first – process information through our senses – get a gut reaction to the speaker and the message he is trying to convey. If the words used are inconsistent with body language, we instinctively put less weight on the words and believe the non-verbal messages being transmitted. For this reason, it is important to be conscious, and in control, of our non-verbal behaviour.

EXERCISE

Consider the three basic behaviour types: *aggressive*, *passive* and *assertive*. Write what would be typical body language posture, movement etc, under the following categories:

Aggressive

Posture	*Gestures*
Facial expression	*Eye contact*
Movement	*Tone of voice*

Passive

Posture	*Gestures*
Facial expression	*Eye contact*
Movement	*Tone of voice*

Assertive

Posture	*Gestures*
Facial expression	*Eye contact*
Movement	*Tone of voice*

COMMENTS

Aggressive body language

In many ways we follow other members of the animal kingdom when we act instinctively – as we do with body language. A typical aggressive *stance* is an erect posture (drawing yourself up to your full height) with hands on hips, elbows pointing out.

In this way we are making ourselves look as large and intimidating as possible – rather like cats with fur on end and tails like brushes, or toads that puff themselves up when challenged.

Facially, all the muscles become tight. There is a taut look about the mouth and often an ambiguous smile that doesn't reach the eyes, which remain stony. In some, a tell-tale sign will be muscles working along the jaw as teeth are gritted. Eyes may be narrowed and there may be a frown or scowl. Any behaviour which puts the other person down is aggressive so, on another level, patronizing 'simpers' can also be seen as aggressive. There may well be a raising of colour – aggressive behaviour can raise the blood pressure!

Movement will be tense and jerky. There may be signs of impatience such as rubbing thighs or tapping feet. The aggressive person may invade your space, standing uncomfortably close. Typically aggressive behaviour is turning or walking away before the other person has had a chance to finish speaking.

Regarding *gestures*, like members of the cat family, we too show our teeth and claws, not perhaps literally, but by jutting our heads forward, pointing or wagging fingers and clenching fists. A dismissive, throw-away gesture of the hand is also aggressive. There may be patronizing touching or patting. There can be short, quick nods of impatience.

Eye contact is usually more intense. Looks will be hard and blinking is reduced. An aggressive person will usually try to outstare the other person.

The *tone of voice* is likely to be either louder and harsher than usual, or sometimes threateningly quiet. Some people talk more slowly, deliberately emphasizing each word. This, of course, is typical of patronizing behaviour. With others, volume and speed of delivery escalate with the level of aggressive behaviour shown. There can also be implied threat or sarcasm.

Passive body language

Research has shown that if people are asked which of two people of the same gender, similar age and identical attire – one with an upright stance; the other round-shouldered – is the boss and which the subordinate, most will assume that the upright figure is in charge. This should tell us something about the *posture* of assertion and success compared with passivity and submission. A slumped appearance is typical of a passive, unassertive person. When seated there is a tendency for the body to curl in on itself. A tight crossing of arms and twining of legs is also characteristic – another 'animal' defence – protecting the soft underside.

A person's passivity is often shown *facially* by a gloomy expression, an over-apologetic or pleading look, or the obvious signs of stress, tension and anxiety, like chewing the lower lip. The chin is drooped towards the chest, shoulders hunched. A raising of colour or actual blushing may occur.

Movement may well be tense and agitated, fidgeting and changing position. Tension may make them clumsy, spilling things, dropping papers. There can be a desire to maintain a physical distance or even to back away from the other person. When seated, they may consciously pull elbows and knees towards the body in a hugging position.

Gestures include clenched hands or a clenching and unclenching nervous mannerism. There can be fiddling with hair, clothes, pens and so on. Often the mouth is covered by the hand while speaking and there will be a lot of face touching. Conversely, in a person who has very low self-esteem, there may be very little movement or gesture – the ultimate in passivity.

Passive people often find it hard to maintain *eye contact*. Their gaze will often be lowered. They may blink more often than is customary. Their eyes may dart about nervously. Again, the converse is sometimes true; the eye contact is almost constant as the passive person hangs on the other person's every word. There is also the disconcerting phenomenon of closing the eyes for long periods of time, literally shutting out the other person. Ostrich like? 'If I can't see him he's less of a threat' perhaps.

The *tone of voice* will usually be quiet – in extreme cases there will be a nervous tremor. Speech may be tentative or hesitant with lots of 'umms', 'uhs' or mumblings. There may be an apologetic whining tone.

Assertive body language

The assertive person has an upright, calm, open *posture* with hands hanging loosely at the sides or in the lap. There will be little crossing of arms and legs, unless in an obviously relaxed manner.

Facial muscles too, will be relaxed, showing sincerity, confidence and responsiveness. The assertive person greets the other with a genuine smile – again, the analogy with the animal kingdom: all primates 'smile' in greeting. Primates also raise and lower their 'eyebrows' almost imperceptibly as a sign of friendly greeting. Try saying 'Hello' to someone keeping your brows absolutely still. You can only do this if you dislike the person you are greeting. These body language messages are usually only registered on a subconscious level, but are very meaningful in interpersonal relationships.

Movement will be steady, regulated and relaxed. An assertive person will tend to lean towards the other person, but will keep the head erect in a responsive rather than a threatening way. They will be comfortable with closer proximity than would a non-assertive person without invading the other's space.

Gestures will be appropriate to the conversation with no excessive or intrusive mannerisms. There is usually much showing of palms – indicating that there is nothing to hide, perhaps?

Eye contact will be direct and regular, showing attention and interest.

The tone of voice will be appropriate to the situation; evenly pitched and steady but easily heard.

Try watching a television programme with the sound turned off. See whether you can understand what's happening, or assess the relationship between interacting people just by watching expression, movement and gesture. You will be surprised how much can be deduced. Actions really do speak louder than words!

KEY POINTS

- Often what people *see* when you talk to them makes a greater impression than what they *hear*.

- Posture, facial expression, eye contact, movements must be appropriate to the situation and congruent with what is being said.

- Be aware of, and try to eliminate, negative – passive or aggressive – body language.

RELATIONSHIPS

Earlier we examined how self-confidence can help you to assert yourself. In fact, if you are self-confident, difficult situations in which you need consciously to assert yourself actually diminish. You are not seen as the easy push-over or victim, so people are more likely to relate to you in a positive way. Self-confidence can be enhanced if you learn how better to relate to people, whoever they are: friends, acquaintances, colleagues, bosses, clients and people you are meeting for the first time – even people with whom you don't usually see eye to eye.

Assertiveness is not about one-off statements when a need arises, with perhaps a few follow-up assertive phrases to reinforce your case. It is a positive, constructive and on-going communication process. During the course of your day you will interact with many people, and in every instance it helps the communication process if you can build some sort of relationship with them – however temporary it might be. You don't have to be best friends with everyone and the relationship can be as fleeting as the duration of a single conversation. People like people who are like themselves, so if you can show – within the first few moments of meeting someone – that you are on their wavelength, they will be more likely to like you, listen to you and respect you. It therefore makes sense to put a little effort into creating a rapport with them. You don't even have to like the person concerned – just act as if you do and you will find communicating with them is a lot easier.

MATCHING

If you are meeting someone for the first time, demonstrate your assertiveness by your confident posture, by smiling, by looking them directly in the eye, and by maintaining an approachable and pleasant demeanour. Learn quickly to identify the sort of language the other person prefers to use. Is their speech formal and serious or do they prefer a more chatty approach? Do they speak slowly, in an unhurried way with pauses in their speech, or do they speak quickly? Is their voice loud or quiet? Whatever their preferred style, adapt your approach accordingly. Choose the sorts of words and phrases that are likely to appeal to them. Quicken or slow down your speech *slightly* to pace theirs. Increase or decrease your own volume a bit to be more in line with theirs. Adjust your voice pitch by a notch to create greater harmony. Changes in your own style need to be subtle and within a range with which you are comfortable. Initially, choose just one aspect and try to create more of an affinity. When this feels quite natural for you, gradually add other matching elements. Try this with someone you already know but with whom you find communication difficult. We all know at least one person with whom we don't gel for some reason. Matching really does help create rapport.

When you use your voice you are displaying several different qualities. Two have been mentioned above: volume and speed of delivery. Can you think of at least three more qualities you can listen for and match when talking with someone? List them below.

1 _____

2 _____

3 _____

4 _____

5 _____

6 _____

COMMENTS

The more of the following you can match, the greater and more effective will be the rapport created.

1 Volume – is their voice soft and quiet or resonant and loud?

2 Speed – how fast or slowly do they speak?

3 Tone – what is conveyed by their tone; do they whine or bluster? Do they sound confident or fearful? Does their tone convey anger or apathy?

4 Rhythm – is their speech punctuated by pauses? Have they got a staccato way of talking? Is their intonation 'melodic' or on a monotone?

5 Pitch – what is their range; is their voice high or low in pitch?

6 Special characteristics – have they got a 'throaty' or husky voice? Be careful with this one because if you match this too obviously – or mimic an accent – it is likely to offend the other person and rapport will be broken.

MIRRORING

Have you noticed that people who get on well together tend to adopt the same body posture when communicating? Watch two people who you know to be friends as they talk with each other. See how they mirror each other's movements as they change position. They often also mirror gestures and mannerisms. This is happening quite unconsciously and naturally. If you want to create rapport with someone, you can use mirroring to good effect. Remember that everything you do is to help build empathy. Overcook it and you will achieve the opposite of your desired effect. You must have respect for yourself and for the other person and use these techniques to aid constructive and positive communication that will benefit you both – never to manipulate or control. For this reason, mirroring must be subtle and within boundaries with which you are comfortable. Alter your position *slightly, slowly and gradually* to be more in tune with the other person's posture.

You can also consider mirroring facial expressions. We have said that an assertive person will have an open, approachable and pleasant demeanour and this should be the case for much of the time. Of course, there will be occasions when your face needs to express specific emotions: sympathy, annoyance, determination and so on, but when establishing a rapport with someone it is helpful sometimes to go part-way towards mirroring that person's own preferred style. For example, if they have a sombre and rather static face, they may find your mobile expressions distracting, and vice versa. Remember that people like people who are like themselves. Modify your expressions slightly to be more in tune with theirs and communication will become easier.

WHY BOTHER TO MATCH AND MIRROR?

'But why should I put myself out and adapt to someone else's style when I may never meet them again, or if I don't even like them anyway?', I hear you say. The reason is that an assertive person will know what they want from an interaction and work towards that goal, at all times respecting the other person's feelings, while not neglecting their own. To achieve a desired outcome where both parties feel happy about the interaction is far easier if you respect and like the other person, and this can be achieved by building rapport. As previously stated, the other person is far more likely to listen to and respect your views if you are displaying a likeness to them. Because the other person is unlikely to adapt to *your* style, if you want movement, it has to be you who leads in this game of matching and mirroring.

However, once you feel that rapport has been established, you can gradually lead the other person in the direction you want them to go by reverting slowly to your own preferred style. If you have been successful in creating an affinity, they will follow your lead and you will find that they will begin, unconsciously, to mirror and match *you*, with their voice, posture, gestures and so on. You can see how you might use this technique to actually train another person to be more assertive and less passive or aggressive.

RELATIONSHIPS WITH RELATIVES

Although this is primarily a book about better management skills within the workplace, it is often far more difficult to be assertive with our nearest and dearest, whether with partners, children, parents or other relatives, so perhaps a few words of advice wouldn't go amiss.

It is probably more difficult to express yourself assertively with, say, your partner, because you have an underlying albeit unconscious belief that whatever you do or say, he or she will understand and accept you 'warts and all'. You may subconsciously feel that they have got to embrace your communication, however ineptly stated on your part. Well, after all, they should instinctively know how you feel, realize where they have been remiss and so on – shouldn't they?! You probably don't go to the trouble to set the scene, choose your words carefully, listen attentively, put yourself in their shoes or any of the other courtesies you would offer a work colleague, your boss or even a comparative stranger. It is hardly surprising, therefore, that communication can become difficult, that 'atmospheres' are created, and that disagreements and sometimes hurt feelings ensue.

In fact, it is equally, if not more, important to practise all of your best assertiveness skills, because relationships with relatives, partners and loved ones should matter the most in your life. It is important to offer praise and encouragement and not take things for granted. You should extend to them the courtesy of your undivided attention and listen attentively to what they have to say. You need to work at rapport too – let them know you are on their side and can understand their point of view (even if you don't agree with it).

Often you will need to assert yourself in what could potentially be a heated conversation. Here are a few tips on what to do and what to avoid doing.

Do:

- Decide what you want to achieve by the conversation. It should result in a win/win situation for you both, and you should both leave the conversation feeling good about yourselves.

- Put yourself in their shoes. How might they feel about the situation? Why might they have behaved in that way?

- Listen attentively, with eyes as well as ears – better to understand their words and emotions.

- Acknowledge strong feelings: 'I see you're annoyed by what I've said' or 'I feel that we are trying to score points off each other'.

- Look for the good in the situation.

- Support their position: 'I think I understand what you're saying'.

- Use phrases such as 'I would prefer it if...', 'I need your help in...', 'It would be useful if...', 'Could you...'. Sometimes it's helpful to preface your request with an empathetic statement such as 'There's something I need to discuss with you' or 'Could we sit down and chat for a moment?'

- Offer praise occasionally: 'You've been really understanding about this' or 'I know you wanted to relax today, so thanks for bearing with me'.

- Allow for alternative viewpoints: 'I realize you may see things differently'.

- Allow for the fact that you may be wrong occasionally – and admit this!

Don't:

- Use inflammatory phrases like 'I don't think you heard me', 'Let me repeat...' or 'If you'll let me finish...'.

- Get hung up on what you feel they *should* have done.

- Feel and act superior.

- Use blaming or judgemental language: 'It was wrong for you to...', 'Why on earth did you...?', 'It's all your fault'.

- Criticize without offering a solution.

- Patronize or conversely revert to child-like behaviour.

This last point is especially important when you need to be assertive with children or with older relatives. Let's first look briefly at communicating with children.

If you listen to how some people talk to children, it is hardly surprising that they get an angry, frustrated or insolent response. If you say something like 'Do it because I say so' or 'Never mind what *I* do, do as I tell you – NOW!', or 'You stupid child!', you may achieve short-term compliance, but lording it over children is never effective in the long term. If you spoke to another adult in that way, they would let you know how they felt about your approach in no uncertain manner – so why should children put up with it? Far better to treat children as viable human beings – individuals with their own feelings, responses, likes and dislikes, perceptions and views about their world.

Assertive communication acknowledges this, instructs, motivates, encourages and reinforces good behaviour. So accentuate the positive. Phrase things in a positive 'Would you …?' way rather than using a negative 'Don't …' approach. Remember that behaviour that is rewarded is repeated, so when a child does something of which you approve, show your endorsement by your words and body language. Enthuse, smile, demonstrate that you are truly pleased: 'That's great. You've done really well!' or 'I was very proud of the way you handled that'. If you can follow this up by giving details of what it was that went so well, or what specifically it was that made you so proud, so much the better. The child will learn and want to replicate the good behaviour.

On the subject of older relatives, if like me you have elderly parents, it is very easy to slip into role reversal mode. Elderly relatives like to feel wanted and needed and also to be pampered on occasion, but speaking down to them in the 'And how are we today' vein goes against the grain with a lot of older people who feel, quite rightly, that they are not being treated on an adult–adult basis or shown a respect deserved by every human being. Ignore the idiosyncrasies that often develop with age and extend the same courtesies to the elderly as you would to any other adult you meet. The words you choose to use are obviously important, but pay especial attention to facial expression and also voice intonation because there lies the clue to others that you are 'talking down' to them.

The other side of the coin is when in the presence of parents you revert to behaving as you did as a teenager or young adult. Communication between you may have been excellent then and if the same style works for you now, so be it. However, where conflict existed between you and your parents, by reverting to old communication patterns, similar disagreements and resentments will resurface. Put into practice all the good assertiveness skills you will have learnt from this book. Self-affirm: 'I am a responsible adult in my own right' (Chapter 3). Listen well and give them your full attention (Chapter 6). Ensure that your body language matches the words you use (Chapter 7). Choose your words and phrases carefully (Chapter 9). Ensure that your tone of voice, etc is appropriate (Chapters 8 and 10). Learn to say 'Yes' to yourself and 'No' to others on occasion (Chapter 11). Re-train your parents to communicate with you on an adult–adult basis.

EXERCISE

Consider the dialogues below. Suggest an alternative assertive response in each case.

a Partner A: 'You didn't tell me you didn't want to go.'
   Partner B: 'You should have known I wouldn't. You
       know how I feel about Alice and Ted.'

b Child: 'Why should I?'
   Parent: 'Because I know what's best for you.'

c Parent: 'Hello stranger.'
   Daughter: 'Yes … er … I'm sorry I've neglected you a bit,
       but you know … er … pressure of work … er … and
       the kids have been playing up.'

d Parent: 'Another mad-cap scheme. It'll be a five-minute
       wonder like the rest of your ideas.'
   Son: 'Typical. You've never supported me in anything I do.'

COMMENTS

There are, of course, no 'correct' responses, but there are many more assertive than those suggested above. In the first instance we will guess that Partner B didn't offer an opinion one way or the other when the meeting with Ted and Alice was suggested. Neither did B let A know how she felt, but assumed that he would guess (by mood, facial expression, body language?) that she didn't like or want to spend time with that couple. If you expect people to read your mind – to know what you want or what you are thinking – you're likely to get nowhere. Faced with the situation, Partner B might have said something like 'I'm sorry; it was a mistake to assume that you knew how I felt. In the future could you ask if it's OK before committing me to an evening out. I don't get on with Alice and Ted, and would rather not go.'

In the second example the parent, instead of treating the child as a reasoning individual, resorts to a 'Because I said so' type of response to his question 'Why should I?', which is in fact a request for information – why he should do whatever it is the parent requested of him. The parent should respond accordingly, eg 'Because it's likely to rain, so you'll need to wear your raincoat to keep you dry' or 'Because Grandma will be disappointed if you don't'.

In the third scenario the parent is trying to spring the guilt trap on her daughter. She should avoid being manipulated in this way by not responding to what is implied, but showing her self-confidence by her demeanour and expression, her calm and assertive manner and saying something like 'Hello Mum, you're looking well. That dress really suits you; is it new?' and continue in this vein until normal conversation begins.

The final example is of a situation where a parent can't relinquish the dominance he had over his child – now a grown man. The response should have been something like, 'I'm sorry you can't see the potential in this Dad, but I have researched it well and I am confident that it will succeed.'

KEY POINTS

- Self-confidence can be enhanced when you learn how better to relate with people.

- You can create a connection with the other person by subtle mirroring or matching.

- Mirroring and matching can also be used to help the other person become less passive or aggressive.

- Use mirroring and matching to create the rapport needed to reach a positive outcome.

WORDS AND PHRASES

By now you will have realized that assertive behaviour is a way of life – a complete philosophy which involves the way you think and feel about yourself and others; the image you portray through non-verbal communication and body language; being able to 'read' others and respond appropriately at different times, with different people in different situations.

Until you think positively, and mirror that thinking with posture, gesture and so on, the best of carefully chosen words will be open to misinterpretation, so having explored those other aspects of assertiveness it's time to look at vocabulary and the construction of assertive statements, questions, requests and directives.

DIRECT, ASSERTIVE COMMUNICATION

Assertive communication means expressing yourself concisely and clearly in a direct, honest and spontaneous way. It also means matching your vocabulary to the person receiving the communication.

This means avoiding technical words, verbal shorthand, acronyms or jargon which are outside the comprehension of the listener. Consider aspects such as education, status and social standing; use language that the other will understand, not which proves how smart or 'superior' you are.

What are the possible consequences of your listener not understanding the words you use?

EXERCISE

List below some of the effects of using language inappropriate to your listener(s).

_____

_____

_____

_____

_____

_____

_____

COMMENTS

Heading your list will possibly be 'they will switch off/stop listening'. This is the least of your worries! Yes, they will, but in the meantime you have also set your relationship back a few notches. It has shown you to be 'different' from them, at another level of knowledge or intellect.

However attentive we are, when we are confronted with a word we don't recognize, we first dredge our brains for similar words which we might understand, or other occasions when we might have heard the word used. We consider the unfamiliar word in context to see if this helps elucidate meaning. By the time we realize that we're never going to understand, the speaker has moved on – we've missed a part of the communication entirely– and it will take a few seconds to tune in again.

One word or piece of jargon you might just get away with, but if you continue to use vocabulary which is unfamiliar to the listener, the gap between speaker and receiver will continue to grow. The listener will not only switch off, but will have a sense of his own ignorance. As this is not a pleasant experience, it will either deflate him – he will feel demoralized, energy levels and listening capacity will fall and self-esteem may suffer – or he will get angry with you, the speaker, for making him feel less knowledgeable. Phrases such as 'pompous prat' are likely to spring to mind!

Of course, an assertive listener would say 'I don't understand' but this is not always possible during a lecture or presentation, for example. The speaker goes away satisfied that she has been heard and understood; the listener(s) feel frustrated, anxious, unsure and generally unhappy with both the communication and the communicator.

The moral of this, of course, is that there is no single appropriate choice of vocabulary. You must choose words with which you are comfortable and which suit the occasion and the recipients of your communication.

There are some principles which apply to every occasion, with each recipient, however, but remember that it's not just the words that are important – intonation and delivery must play their part in effective, assertive communication.

BE DIRECT

State exactly what you feel or think; don't rely on your actions to tell the story. We often assume – especially when the interaction is with someone to whom we are close – that they will know instinctively what we want, feel or need. For example, don't presume because you are slamming around in an obvious 'mood' that other people will know *why* you are put out or angry. They *may* have some idea, but unless you state clearly 'I am annoyed because ...' or 'I feel let down because ...' you can't be *sure* that they know why you are annoyed, disappointed or whatever. If they don't know exactly what the problem is, how can they begin to fix it?

TACKLE THE PROBLEM NOT THE PERSON

There's a difference between 'Why can't you clear up after yourself' and 'Please tidy this workbench'. The former implies a character defect; the latter requires a solution to a problem. You can imagine for yourself the impact each statement might have on the recipient.

DEAL WITH SPECIFICS, NOT GENERALIZATIONS

Compare 'You're always late' with 'Why were you late again this morning?' It's unlikely that someone is always anything! Be specific about the problem; don't accuse, state facts.

DON'T OVER-APOLOGIZE

'Honestly, I can't apologize enough – I'm most dreadfully sorry ...'

Yes, you *can* apologize enough. *Once* is enough if sincerely said and in an assertive manner. However, we tend to apologize *for* everything and *to* anything let alone anyone. We bump into a door and apologize to it! How often do we say things like 'Sorry, but I can't work late tonight' when we are not sorry at all? 'No, I've another appointment; I can't work late tonight' is far more direct, accurate and secure from further debate. Be selective and sparing with your 'sorries'.

DON'T GIVE EXCESSIVE EXPLANATIONS

You may feel that a brief reason for a request or refusal, or a short explanation of a statement softens what could otherwise be a blunt message. This is fine if you don't go over the top with justifications, or become defensive. However, often we do all the wrong things for the right reasons. We assume that we are protecting the other person's feelings when in reality we could be confusing or upsetting them.

Example: A friend asks whether you could look after her dog for the weekend. You reply:

> *'Well, I'd love to help, and if there was anything else ... but Pongo! It's not that I don't like him but his fur upsets me. I mean, he's a lovely dog – as dogs go – but I can't get on with them you see. They make me itch and after a while my breathing gets affected ...'*

Do you begin to get the picture? By now the poor dog owner feels responsible for your asthmatic suffering; is wondering how often you have suffered in silence before; is recalling with dismay the occasions she has let Pongo jump all over you; is wondering if she is bathing Pongo enough ... and so on.

'I've got an allergy to dog hair so no, I can't look after Pongo for you' should suffice. As with every aspect of effective interpersonal communication, the situation and the individual concerned will dictate how much or little needs to be added to your direct assertive statement.

TAKE OWNERSHIP OF YOUR MESSAGE

Have the confidence to use 'I' statements. Rather than, 'Don't you think it would be a good idea to research this further?' take ownership of the idea: 'I think more research should be put into this.'

The first statement could be seen as condescending or patronizing and, as such, aggressive. It might be met with a curt 'No, I don't', and you can see how that conversation might escalate. The 'I' statement, while giving the other person the opportunity to accept or reject the suggestion, takes responsibility for individual opinion and comes across as more direct and confident.

Opinions stated as facts can also be taken as aggressive: 'As I'm sure you'll agree, the only sensible thing to do is to amalgamate.'

The first part of the statement, 'As I'm sure you'll agree', makes an assumption, which, if not the case, requires an assertive denial. It can also be seen as patronizing, rather like 'As you know…' prefixes to statements. It takes a confident person to say, 'Well, actually, no – I don't know …'.

To return to the example above, '… the only sensible thing to do is to amalgamate' is an opinion but stated as a fact. What does the word 'sensible' imply about the person who dares to disagree with the speaker? An assertive person would take responsibility for his opinion, 'I think the best option would be to amalgamate.' Implicit in this is respect for your own opinion and respect for others who may hold different views.

Another reason for using 'I' rather than 'you' statements is to assert that you take responsibility for your own thoughts, feelings and needs. For example, if you were to ask 'Do you like this design?' on the one hand it gives the other person the opportunity to give an unbiased opinion, but it could also suggest that you are not confident enough in your own judgement to come out and say 'I like this design' or conversely, 'I feel that this design needs reworking'.

A direct assertive message means that we speak for ourselves – 'I need …', 'I feel hurt when …', 'I am not going to …', 'I will … but only if ...'. By using 'I' statements to express feelings and emotions, you give the other person very little ground for debate. They might argue with tangibles, but no one can argue with how you actually feel.

EXERCISE

Rewrite the following as 'I' statements:

'You make me so angry when you don't listen to me.'

'It's generally agreed that voluntary redundancy is the answer.'

'We don't smoke during meals in our house.'

COMMENTS

Try something like:

'I get angry when you walk away without hearing me out.'

'I believe that voluntary redundancy is the answer.'

'I'd rather you didn't smoke at meal times.'

HONESTY

... honesty in the sense of being true to yourself, and in assertively expressing what you really feel.

Being true to yourself isn't easy because conditioning has given you a set of 'should' rules. Go against these 'shoulds' and 'ought tos' and guilty feelings ensue. True? And isn't being true to yourself, in this context, a bit selfish?

Looked at another way, isn't it more important to be in control and in charge of your own life? Honesty entails asserting your needs and feelings *as they are*, not as other people feel they should be. Your life shouldn't be controlled by 'ought tos', value judgements or role restrictions.

This one takes a lot of practice, not least to convince *yourself*, and to stop the angst every time you assert your right to be you. However, after a few honest assertions, I promise it will get easier each time you consciously take control of your own life. Try statements such as 'Yes, I do take my responsibilities as a mother seriously, but my work is important to me too' or 'I understand why you feel that I shouldn't be upset by this, but I am' or 'I accept that it seems irrational, but I worry when I lend my car'.

Remember the basic rights listed in Chapter 4. Provided you respect the other person's rights honestly to express feelings and needs, you should have no problem in assertively allowing the same right for yourself. Ultimately, everyone will gain. As Polonius said to his son Laertes in Shakespeare's *Hamlet*:

'This above all: to thine own self be true,

And it must follow, as the night the day,

Thou canst not then be false to any man.'

DIRECTIVES AND REQUESTS

A teacher in a primary school found she had a basic communication problem with one of the children who came from, and was being brought up within, a different culture. When she asked 'Would you like to close that window for me' he said 'No, thank you' – a perfectly logical response to a poorly phrased request. He was not being rude; he merely had a less sloppy command of the English language than most of us, and a background which believed in giving spontaneous, honest responses.

EXERCISE

Rewrite the following as (a) assertive *requests* and (b) assertive *directives*.

'Would you mind telephoning head office for me?'

'Why don't you open and distribute the mail before making everyone's coffee?'

'I need this report typed by 5 pm.'

COMMENTS

The requests in each case will begin with the words 'Will you' or better still, 'Will you please...'. The directives will be more emphatic; for example, 'Please telephone head office for me' or 'Please open and distribute...'.

There was a story quoted in a book I've read – I can't remember which one, so won't be able to credit the author. It told the rather embarrassing tale of a man who asked his female companion, 'Would you marry me?' 'Oh yes!' she replied – and rushed home to tell her family and friends that she was engaged, to the horror of the man who had asked a grammatical and factual question but, unfortunately, a hypothetical one. What he should have added was 'Would you marry me *if I were free to ask you*'. He was in fact already married, but wanted to test his girlfriend's fidelity. She had mistaken the meaning of 'would' for 'will'.

This proves three things: selective listening will be a problem in any conversation – we hear what we want to hear; sometimes you can be *too* succinct, some detail is necessary; and however carefully you choose your words you must check that the other person has understood your meaning!

SPONTANEITY

Perhaps the most difficult aspect of assertiveness to master is spontaneity because, as we have discussed, most often our gut reaction is either avoidance and repression, or confrontation and aggression. Many people, unskilled in assertiveness, are accommodating and passive up to a point, and then, when the situation requires more pro-active behaviour, begin to function on a more aggressive level. The assertive option seldom enters the equation. This is because assertiveness isn't instinctive behaviour; it doesn't come naturally – it's a skill which has to be learnt, then practised until it becomes as second nature as the other options.

In fact, we should aim for spontaneous assertive reaction in most circumstances. As a manager, you may feel that either accommodating or aggressive behaviour has suited your purposes because it matches your organization's style of operating. As we have seen, there will be times in the workplace where non-assertive behaviour *is* an appropriate response.

However, effective communication and strong interpersonal relationships are essential to good leadership, and there are areas at work, especially when dealing with problem people or situations, where the assertive option will obtain better results.

Assertiveness is a choice of behaviour and one which should be added to every manager's repertoire. It will benefit you both inside and outside the workplace.

EXERCISE

Give some thought to why immediate assertive self-expression would be important to you in the following situations:

1 Your partner agrees, on your behalf, that you should both attend a dinner party with people you personally don't like.

2 Your boss tells you that he intends to introduce a radical new procedure in your department.

3 You are waiting to be served in the canteen. A colleague comes in, sees a friend of hers queuing directly ahead of you, so joins her to chat. It is obvious that she will queue jump – and you are in a hurry.

4 A co-worker with whom you share an office has begun to display a distracting habit, such as tapping a pen on the desk while thinking, or whistling tunelessly, or punctuating his conversation with the filler 'do you know what I mean?' to the point of annoyance.

5 Lately, every time you ask your clerk if you can see her in your office, she says 'be with you in a minute'. It appears that she continues with her work until she finds a convenient gap to fit you into her busy schedule.

COMMENTS

Spontaneous assertive self-expression is important in all instances if you are to avoid the fight or flight response, ie either begin to seethe and over-react, or withdraw from the situation and the person. Both reactions can escalate, resulting in misunderstandings, anger or hurt feelings on either or both sides. You will withdraw more and more from the person, or eventually explode, usually over something minor and unrelated to the original annoyance.

If you don't respond assertively to nip difficult situations in the bud, you are likely, therefore, to expend energy in an unproductive way, potentially damaging relationships – and your health and well-being.

KEY POINTS

- Effective communication involves expressing yourself clearly in a direct, honest and spontaneous way.
- Choose words and phrases carefully to construct assertive statements, requests, questions and directives.

POWER

This chapter asks you to consider two meanings of the word *power*: power of delivery or the amount of force needed for you to get your message across, and the concept of power over others and how you can use or abuse it.

CONFIDENT DELIVERY

Why is it that some people have a seemingly natural ability to command attention and respect when they speak? What is it that makes others listen and pay attention to their words? It isn't necessarily a question of status, or the content of what they say. Such people often don't speak 'Oxford' English, express themselves using perfect grammatical constructions, or even have perfect diction. What they *do* have is resonance. Such people tend to have melodious, rich voices and to use the lower end of their voice range. Observe and listen to others. People who speak quickly and breathily in a high-pitched voice do not appear as assertive as those who speak more slowly using deeper voice tones. The lower pitch conveys control and confidence.

It would be ridiculous to suggest that from now on you growl your way through life by self-consciously lowering the tone of your voice, but you can begin to achieve greater resonance by practising the way you breathe. Try this. Stand in front of a mirror breathing naturally. Now draw a deep breath. Does your chest expand? Do your shoulders rise? I thought so. You are breathing 'high', using your rib rather than your abdominal muscles. Try again, this time putting your hands across your stomach. When you breathe in, consciously keep your shoulders lowered and fill your lungs from the abdomen – you will feel your stomach expanding. If you practise abdominal breathing, you will be utilizing all, not just the top, of your lungs, which in itself must be beneficial. You will also be engaging your diaphragm more, and this in turn will access the lower end of your voice range and add resonance to your voice, conveying more authority.

VOLUME AND INTONATION

Words delivered in a monotone soon become just that – monotonous! Your delivery will need light and shade if you want to keep the attention of your listener. Assertive delivery requires smooth-flowing, resonant inflection; the voice will be relaxed with enough volume to be heard distinctly without being overpowering.

However, there are some occasions when assertive behaviour requires a little more power than generally recommended for everyday conversation. If you were to see a small child about to put her hand into an activated food-processor, it would be inappropriate to say, in a low-pitched, relaxed way, 'I'd prefer you not to put your hand into that food-processor.' Assertive, yes; practical, no! Obviously, there are occasions – when someone's personal safety is at risk, for instance – when more force of delivery is required.

The *content* of the communication doesn't have to become aggressive, however. In the above example, a loud, strident 'NO' to stop the action immediately and demand attention, followed by a forceful explanation of why that was a dangerous thing to do, would be an appropriate response, whereas 'Stop! Don't do that you stupid child!' would be an inappropriate (though human and understandable) one. The whole child is labelled as 'stupid' rather than the action itself being criticized. Appropriate volume and intonation *without aggressive put-downs* will give the other person the message that you mean business.

Another common failing is to attack with a sledgehammer when a feather would have done the job. In other words, when we are tense, overworked or just plain irritable, we often respond with a force totally inappropriate to the situation.

To give an example: you are immersed in an interesting article in the Sunday papers. Your partner is scanning the supplement and constantly interrupts, reading aloud witty bits and snippets. It's breaking your concentration and getting on your nerves. You say nothing, but when she then asks something which requires a response, like 'Do you want a coffee?' you snap 'No, I *don't*; we only had one half an hour ago. You must be slopping at the edges!'

The intensity of the response reflects your annoyance at the previous interruptions and is certainly unfair, and totally inappropriate to the situation. (It might also reflect irritation at your own lack of assertion when earlier you should have said something like, 'Can you read that to me later? This article is a bit complex and I need to concentrate.')

There are occasions in everyone's life, social and business, when the skill of using appropriate volume and force needs to be practised. For example, when you have given an assertive request in clear, level tones and that request is ignored, you have two choices: give up the fight and put up with the situation as it is, or make your request again, this time with a little more force. If you take the latter course, you could either change the wording of your request, making it a directive which will give the message more 'punch' and/or increase volume, altering intonation to match the emotion behind the delivery, for example:

'Will you please tidy this work station.'
(request ignored)

'Please *tidy* this *work station*.'
(request ignored)

'I want you to clear this work station – *now!*'

As requests move to directives, commands, indications of what will happen if your demands are not met and so on, statements are expressed with increased verbal and non-verbal intensity. Volume and force of delivery will increase, posture and facial expression will all convey more force.

EXERCISE

For this exercise you really need the help of a colleague or friend – someone you can trust to give constructive feedback.

Consider the following situations. Role-play each beginning with an assertive statement. Ask your colleague to ignore you or give some sort of excuse rather than agree to your request. Persist, increasing verbal and non-verbal intensity.

1 You see that a colleague is using your personal calculator. As the calculator was in your briefcase, you know that she has gone through your property. You feel this is an invasion of privacy and don't want it to happen again.

2 You are trying to watch a TV documentary. Your partner/son/daughter/flatmate is playing loud music in another room. You need the volume turned down in order to enjoy your programme.

COMMENTS

Ask your colleague to give constructive feedback on whether your initial statement was, in fact, assertive, and whether follow-up statements reflected more force by choice of words, volume, intonation and facial expression *without resorting to aggressive behaviour.*

PROJECTION

You may find yourself in other types of situation where force of delivery is required – ones which are not so charged with emotion, however. If you have to give a presentation or address a large group of people, you will need to acquire yet another skill – projection. Here you require volume without shouting, but with plenty of intonation to give light and shade to your communication.

If I may indulge in an anecdote at this point: newscasters reading from autocues should pay attention to intonation as it is all too easy to put the wrong emphasis on words when reading from a script. A local news item about the police looking at different ways of handling emergency telephone calls was reported as follows:

'The police are anxious because people *can't get through.'*

The emphasis on the word 'people' implied that perhaps plants, animals and aliens had no trouble at all connecting with the local police, whereas people had. Those of you who read from notes when making presentations – take heed!

POSITION AND STATUS

Power can be tangible and visible to another before any words are spoken. We have discussed briefly how bearing and the way we dress can affect others' perception of us. How we greet others, the handshake we give (and who offers a hand first), the spacial difference between individuals, the orientation – whether face-to-face, right angle, side-by-side positioning – the layout of rooms, choice of furniture and so on, all reflect status and power, and will influence passive, aggressive or assertive behaviour in self and others.

Consider this scenario. Bill and John meet in the office corridor.

'John! I haven't seen you for ages; how's business?'
Handshake, Bill offering right hand, placing left on John's shoulder.

'Business is fine … etc.'
John talks for a while about his new project.

'Great talking to you John; we must have a round of golf together again sometime.'
Bill backs away, turning to leave the conversation.

Of the two, who is the managing director of the company and who the visiting supplier wanting to do business?

In this hypothetical situation, it could be either, of course. It might depend on the character of the two individuals, one being naturally more gregarious and demonstrative than the other. However, Bill is more likely to be the MD at home on his own territory, and John the visiting supplier, wanting to do business with the organization. The clues are who initiated the handshake; the physical touching; who indicated that the conversation was at an end by backing or turning away. This subtle, non-verbal communication helps establish relationships – in this case dominance (my territory; you want something from me, not the other way around).

Similarly, power can be used or abused by recognizing acceptable social distance. An assertive person will not invade another's personal space. We've all been in the position where someone stands just that bit too close, and for whatever reason, it is threatening and we feel the need to back away.

I happen to be physically small – I believe 'vertically challenged' is a politically correct phrase! It is difficult to be assertive when others are towering over me. A way to redress this balance is to sit, inviting the other person to do likewise. Although I am still smaller, if we are both seated on similar height chairs, assertion is far more easy. If I were to remain standing, while the other person sits, I would put myself in a position of dominance and therefore, in theory, be the more powerful. (If the other person declines to sit, I get back on my feet and make the best of it, of course.)

You can see that there are occasions when use (or abuse) of power through non-verbal communication could be useful, but an assertive person will always try to create an environment where there is equality of opportunity to communicate 'from a level playing field'.

EXERCISE

Consider the following scenarios. In each case, which is likely to create an atmosphere where assertive communication can take place? Think about the pros and cons of each setting.

1 a A training room is set up in traditional classroom style with chairs in staggered rows. The trainer's desk is at the front, as is the flipchart.

  b A training room is set up with chairs in a circle. The trainer's chair and flipchart form part of this circle.

  c A training room is set up with chairs in a horseshoe shape, the trainer's table and flipchart in the 'jaws' of the horseshoe.

2 a You are called to see your boss. She is sitting behind her desk and invites you to sit on a chair, similar to hers, at the side of her desk at right angles to her.

b You are called to see your boss. She is sitting behind her desk, but gets up as you come in and moves to easy chairs in the corner of her room, indicating that you both should sit in these.

c You are called to see your boss. She is sitting behind her desk and invites you to sit on a chair, lower than and directly facing hers, placed very close to her desk.

3 **a** The interviewing panel are sitting behind a large table with their backs to the window. You, the interviewee, are invited to sit some distance away from them, on a chair in the centre of the room.

b The interviewing panel are sitting on easy chairs set in a curve. The window is to their left. You are asked to sit in a similar chair, facing them, with just a coffee table between you.

COMMENTS

If you are ever asked to run a training session for your team, the layout of the room is important as it will dictate the atmosphere of the event.

In *scenario 1(a)* sitting behind a desk in schoolroom style will create a barrier – and thus a distance – between you and your team. This layout is not conducive to the sharing of ideas and equality of communication. If the size of the group demands rows of chairs, always come out from behind your barrier – however safe you might feel behind it – to lessen the 'you versus them' atmosphere. Consider the effect you will make if you sit on a chair out front, stand, perch on the table, pace up and down the room etc. Which looks most assertive? Why do other postures appear non-assertive?

The *second layout* described is perfect for a session where participation is encouraged. It's rather like King Arthur's round table where all are equal participants in the event. Everyone can make eye contact. Remember the importance of using the same height and type of chair for everyone. Basically, anyone at a higher level sends the non-verbal message of power.

The *third option* is presently the most typical layout for training sessions in that the importance of eye contact is acknowledged, while trainer 'activity' can take place within the jaws of the horseshoe. By activity I mean the movement of the trainer as he alternates between using flipchart, OHP and other visual aids, and joining the group for discussion.

Scenario 2 has three options. The orientation at right angles is the normal relaxed position with which *most British* people are comfortable. (Other cultures favour different positions for relaxed communication.) Provided that chairs are of similar type and height, this set-up would be conducive to assertive dialogue and has the additional benefit of both participants being able to look at documents, etc, on the desk.

The *second option* is the most appropriate of all if the communication is to proceed on an equal footing.

The *third option* just asks for conflict. At best it demands dominance of the boss and subjection by you! In this situation, face-to-face orientation is aggressive and confrontational. The height and position of chairs is designed to make you feel uncomfortable and at a distinct disadvantage. Interestingly, this type of over-close, face-to-face orientation means the exact opposite to aggressive confrontation when adopted by two people who are emotionally close. Invariably, they will choose restaurant seats directly opposite, rather than side by side or at right angles to each other.

The *third scenario* – the interview – is one with which we are all familiar from one perspective or the other. The first example is sure to make the interviewee feel ill at ease. The panel have the protection of their barrier – the table – whereas the interviewee is totally exposed with nothing behind which to hide his shaking knees!

After some time looking at people against the light, their features will begin to blur – even vanish – and all images will take on an unreal, shimmering effect. I'm sure you've been in this situation, so know what I mean! Sitting alone, in the middle of the room, with back exposed to the unseen void behind is also intimidating. In short, if you are holding an interview and want to put the other person at their ease in order to facilitate assertive dialogue, all of the above must be avoided.

The *second example*, however, creates a relaxed atmosphere in which the interviewee is invited to meet the panel on equal terms. No one has the window disadvantage. The coffee table is low enough not to be a barrier to communication, but creates appropriate spacial distance (imagine a smallish room without the table – it 'feels' less comfortable). The table also allows somewhere for papers to be deposited. Rather than sitting in a line as suggested by the first example, the interviewing panel are here sitting in a curve so that they too can engage in eye contact and relaxed communication.

The point of this section is not to suggest that you can use spacial distance, orientation, furnishings and fittings to achieve your own ends; rather it is to emphasize that this aspect of non-verbal communication is another vitally important factor in sending your assertive message. Get one part of the equation wrong and your effectiveness will suffer.

KEY POINTS

- The power of your words – volume, tone and intensity – should fit the situation.
- Non-verbal communication should emphasize the intensity you intend.
- Position and status can be used or abused. An assertive person will always try to create and maintain a 'level playing field'.

YES AND NO

As we've progressed through this book we've gradually added more and more aspects of assertiveness training. The next three chapters begin to pull it all together, expanding on some themes already mentioned.

MAKING AND REFUSING REQUESTS

In the last chapter we looked at making requests, adding more force to the communication if necessary for results. It should go without saying that before making a request you should really know what it is you want, yet often this is one of the most difficult things to get to grips with. Right at the start of the book we talked about really knowing yourself, and this is an essential element in expressing needs and preferences, setting goals, and in saying 'Yes' and 'No' for, and to, yourself.

We also talked about actively listening to others. You must also learn to listen to your own inner voice which is forever having arguments with your gut! Your gut reaction tells you one thing, but your inner voice keeps catastrophizing – 'but what if ...?' and pricking your conscience with all the things you should and ought to do rather than going with the flow.

So you've decided what it is that you want; you now need to convey this assertively ... to whom? The person who can do something about your wants or needs. Stating the obvious you might think, but we often tell other people our needs, in a manipulative sort of way, in the hope that they will somehow accurately relay the message to the person concerned.

For example, the member of staff who comes to you complaining that she doesn't understand her pay slip, when she should be asking for clarification from the relevant person in the accounts department; or the person who complains bitterly and loudly to no one in particular about someone queue-jumping when he should confront the person concerned and request that he join the line of people waiting. Admit it – how often have you complained about your son/daughter/spouse/colleague/boss to someone else in the hope that miraculously your needs will be realized, rather than grasping the nettle and assertively saying 'I would prefer it if ...' or 'Would you please help me with ...'.

Which brings us to the 'how' of making an assertive request. Make a positive 'I' statement which clearly and concisely expresses your need, want or preference. Ensure that your tone of voice, volume and non-verbal communication appropriately reflect your strength of feeling about the issue.

EXERCISE

Replace the following non-assertive statements with assertive requests:

1 'How can I study with you hovering around? Give me some space!'

2 'Would you mind working overtime on Tuesday?'

3 'If only Andrew would check his work before handing it in – it would save us all a lot of time.'

4 '... *I'm* telling this story!'

5 'I'm not very happy with the arrangements.'

COMMENTS

Try something like:

1 'I need some quiet time, alone, to study.'

2 'Will you please work overtime on Tuesday?'

3 'Andrew, will you please check your work for errors before passing it on to me.'

4 'Let me finish ...'

5 'I'd prefer to be met at the airport terminal.'

You have a basic right to ask for what you want but remember, the other person also has the right to refuse. The bonus is that by making an assertive expression of need or feelings, at least you have had the strength of character positively to state your position, and others will know how you feel and where they stand with you. It will serve you well in future communication with them.

BROKEN RECORD TECHNIQUE

Besides refusing your request outright, there are other options which are open to the other person which you need to consider. They could agree immediately (and you've rehearsed all your persuasive follow-up lines and now won't be able to use them!). They could prevaricate, argue, become aggressive, or offer excuses why they can't agree to your request.

You have several options. You could shelve the issue (the non-assertive response). If the situation demands it, you could use more verbal and non-verbal force as discussed in the last chapter, or you could adopt the 'Broken Record' technique whereby you keep repeating your message until the other person accepts your point of view. This, too, may need more 'muscle' as you progress in the dialogue, but in theory you should be able to maintain an assertive, relaxed tone and volume as you persistently keep to your point.

Example

Jean has forewarned Angela, a junior manager, that she needs an important report typed up in draft form by Tuesday (it's now Monday) so that it can be faxed to regional heads for comment, amendment or approval. She takes her handwritten draft to Angela. The dialogue goes as follows:

Jean: Angela – here's the report on alternative resourcing I mentioned to you. I need it by lunchtime tomorrow.

Angela: I'll do the best I can Jean, but a rush job has come in. All the typists are working on it. I doubt I'll be able to get it to you before Wednesday.

Jean: The final report has to be typed and ready for distribution at Friday's meeting. I need the draft typed by 1pm tomorrow to give regional heads a chance to comment before finalization.

Angela: Well, why can't you e-mail them your handwritten draft? My team are really busy; I can't promise to get your work back to you on time.

Jean: I understand that you have a problem with your team's workload, but I need this report typed and on my desk by 1pm tomorrow, as agreed.

Angela: Why can't you get one of the central typists to do it for you? Or couldn't you use agency typists?

Jean: If you can arrange that, yes. Provided I get an accurately typed copy of this draft by lunchtime tomorrow, that will be fine.

Angela: (Sighing). All right Jean, leave it with me. I'll see what I can do.

Jean: So you will get this draft typed and back with me by lunchtime tomorrow?

Angela: Yes, OK.

Jean: Thanks Angela.

This dialogue does not strictly follow the steps of tight Broken Record technique, where you stick to your guns no matter what, repeating your request over and over until it is understood and acted upon. It does, perhaps, more accurately reflect the type of technique which most people would be happy to practise, in that it allows reasons for the request and added detail where it helps your cause. It recognizes the other person's position – Jean showed that she had paid attention to what Angela said – but ignores irrelevant questions which are intended to sidetrack you from your objective. Close the interaction by reiterating your assertive statement and getting agreement.

All of the above dialogue could take place using a calm, pleasant but firm tone of voice. In a potentially stressful situation such as this, it would have been so easy to lose emotional control, become accusatory, demand to know whose 'rush job' was important enough to take priority over yours, and so on.

Broken Record is a technique most usually associated with saying 'No'. The principles are much the same as those demonstrated above. First, be sure in your own mind about what you want or don't want. State your case clearly and concisely, wherever possible using the word 'No' in your refusal, to leave the other person in no doubt about your meaning. Give only appropriate embellishments to your statements – a brief reason for your refusal or an apology, if you are genuinely sorry, for not being able to agree to their request. The key is to be empathetic, but persistent.

Reflect back to the other person that you have heard and understood them, but nevertheless you intend to stand by your position. The other person will give reasons why you should do as they want, try to show you why your stance is illogical, will use pleading, sulking and other means of emotional blackmail to make you feel guilty for refusing; to make you give in and accede to their wishes. You have to decide whether you can be flexible on the issue and work together towards a mutually acceptable compromise, or stick to your guns however many assertive refusals it takes.

Let's look at the above dialogue again, this time with Angela using Broken Record.

Jean: Angela – here's the report on alternative resourcing I promised you. I need it by lunchtime tomorrow.

Angela: The situation's changed since I told you that would be possible – sorry, Jean; I was about to phone you – but a rush job for the MD has to take priority. No, I won't be able to get your report typed by midday tomorrow.

Jean: What? Why should the MD be able to pull rank like this? I told you about my report and you assured me that my work would be done!

Angela: I understand why you are annoyed. However, I have to decide my team's workload, and the MD's work takes priority so no, we won't be able to get your draft typed by tomorrow.

Jean: Well, what am I supposed to do? You know why I need this tomorrow – so that I can e-mail it through to the regions. I'm disappointed in you. How could you let me down like this!

Angela: I could arrange for agency typists to do the work. I'll phone and see if they can meet your deadline if that helps.

Jean: ... and we all know the quality of work they produce! I'd rather do the typing myself. No, you said you'd do the work – this just isn't on!

Angela: Jean, I'm sorry you feel let down, but no, my team can't get your report typed by tomorrow lunchtime.

Forget the rights and wrongs of the situation for a moment – yes, I expect you sympathize with Jean – but occasions do arise when a senior officer's work, or work of more importance and urgency, has to take priority. Angela politely stood her ground, apologized as appropriate to the situation, acknowledged Jean's emotions – yet persisted in her refusal to meet her demands. She offered a possible solution – a workable compromise – which Jean chose not to accept, so she reverted to her Broken Record method of refusal.

One point to remember: when you say 'No' you are refusing a request, not rejecting the person. Keep this in mind; conduct the interaction with respect for the other person, while not neglecting your own rights, and you will feel less guilty about refusing. Bear this in mind also when *you* are refused a request. The other person is saying 'No' to that particular situation, on that occasion, and is not rejecting you as a person.

EXERCISE

Here you will need the help of a friend or colleague. Ask her/him to choose from the following situations and role-play the person making the request. Your task is to refuse steadfastly, using the Broken Record technique, reasserting your message calmly, remembering that the force of your delivery, your attitude and emotional control are vital in getting across the assertive message. If you think it appropriate you might eventually offer an alternative, acceptable to you both. If the suggestion is rejected, return to Broken Record.

Ask your friend or colleague to use as many persuasive techniques as possible to make you give in and say 'Yes' to the request. Given below are opening lines for the interaction, lines which should be spoken by your colleague.

1 *The scene*: You know you have been neglecting your social contact with colleagues from work, but tonight you want to go home and watch a film on the TV.

   A colleague says: 'How about going out for a drink tonight, after work?'

2 *The scene*: It's Saturday, fine weather, and you have planned to indulge in your favourite hobby.

   Your partner says: 'Can you look after the children today?'

3 *The scene*: You are working to full capacity, but have heard rumours that management do not intend to replace posts lost through natural wastage.

   Your boss says: 'I'd like you to add Wiltshire and Dorset to your territory.'

COMMENTS

Ask your colleague to give you feedback on the following points:

- Was your voice calm and firm?
- Were words, delivery and body language compatible?
- Was the word 'No' actually said ever? Once or twice? At every appropriate assertion?
- Did you give sufficient reason for your refusal or did you tend to overjustify your case?
- Did you say 'sorry' at all? Was the apology sincerely meant/ appropriate? Did you over-apologize?
- Did you smile at all? At appropriate times or through embarrassment?
- Did you offer an alternative, workable compromise?
- If this was rejected, did you return to your Broken Record refusal?

Every assertiveness training course produces the question 'What happens when two assertive people meet, both using the Broken Record technique. Isn't there stalemate?' If there were, it would soon cease to be an assertive interaction and become an aggressive locking of horns! Of course, assertive people would show a respect for each other's needs and adopt the techniques described to reach a win–win solution. Each would know exactly what they wanted; each would know how flexible they would be prepared to be. They would listen and question well to ascertain where differences lie, where needs might dovetail. They would discuss options for resolving the problem to produce a win–win solution and, if all else failed, agree to disagree without hurting, or feeling hurt or offended by the other.

This chapter has concentrated on interactions with other people, expressing needs and preferences, making and refusing requests. It is also crucial to your self-development to listen to that inner voice telling you what you *really* want to do, or *truly* don't want to do. You must learn to say 'Yes' and 'No' to yourself, act on these feelings and become comfortable doing so.

For example, I *should* begin to write Chapter 12 as soon as I've finished here, but it's the first day of November and the sun is shining on this warm Indian Summer day. I *want* to take my dogs for a walk in the country lanes so that we can all make the most of this climatic bonus. So, I'm going to ignore those 'shoulds' and 'oughts' on this occasion and say 'yes' to myself – see you in Chapter 12!

KEY POINTS

- Recognize and use 'I' ownership statements to express your needs or preferences, and in making direct and clear requests.
- Listen to your inner voice and learn how to say 'No'. Be empathetic, but firm and persistent.

PROBLEM PEOPLE

Let's face it – *we're* not the problem are we? It's the other people. If only he were more considerate, or less angry, or more motivated; if she listened more, criticized less and stopped whinging all the time, the world would be a better place!

I hope it goes without saying that we *all* need to look to our own behaviour – put our own houses in order – and that is what assertive behaviour choice is all about. It's learning to recognize and deal with your own negative feelings in an appropriate way. As we've seen, there will be times when accepting, accommodating or aggressive behaviour is appropriate but, increasingly, as you feel more at ease with assertive behaviour, you will naturally opt for the assertive approach.

So how do we cope, assertively, with the myriad of problems we might face through negative behaviour of others? Basically, we use the skills already outlined, adapting them effectively to deal with specific situations.

To recap: problem people can create stress situations, so use a relaxation technique to calm you down and relax the muscles.

A quick but intense clenching of the fists while breathing in, followed by a conscious 'letting go' as you unclench, relax, and breathe out, will help.

Remember positive thinking. Whatever is thrown at you (not literally we hope!) you can and will handle it. Remember the other person's rights, but do not neglect your own. Make sure you are sending an appropriate message through your body language. Choose vocabulary with which you are comfortable and that the other person will understand. You are now in the right frame of mind to begin the interaction.

THE IRATE

When people get angry they get an adrenalin rush. A situation occurs that provokes a 'fight or flight' response and if the person affected tends towards the aggressive, the 'fight' reaction will win. The adrenalin produces energy, and that energy has to expend itself. If your actions or words happen to be the cause of the anger, or you just happen to be in the wrong place at the wrong time, it will be up to you to defuse the situation.

Meet aggression with aggression and the situation will escalate and achieve little except raised blood pressure and bad feeling. If your natural reaction is to rise to the bait, you need to recognize this and deal with it. Remind yourself that the anger is not directed at your personality – the heart of your being – however personal it may sound. The anger may be about something you've done or not done, or a stance you have taken, but you – as a person – are still a responsible individual with rights. Try to distance yourself from the immediacy of the outburst – step outside the situation – and observe and listen objectively. Don't fuel the anger by adding your own 'two pence worth'!

In the past it was recommended that when you decide to intervene or respond to the angry person you should do so using a quiet, composed voice. This may have a calming effect on the other person, but unless his anger has already started to abate, it may well further incense him. Have you ever wanted to have a rattling good argument with someone who steadfastly refuses to respond? Isn't it frustrating? Doesn't it make you even more angry? Try this instead. Remember matching, mirroring, pacing and leading described in Chapter 8. I'm not suggesting that you match the other person's anger or mirror his angry gestures, but 'up' your volume and pitch a little to be more in line with his. Acknowledge that the anger is there: 'I see that you're really angry – I would be too if I were in your position...'. Gradually drop your pitch and decrease your volume as you proceed to defuse the situation. You will find that the other person will subconsciously recognize that you are empathizing with him and will eventually follow your lead and communicate in a more rational way. You may have to wait a while until the storm begins to blow itself out, but by pacing his anger, then leading him into quieter waters by non-judgemental acknowledgement of his feelings, you can go on to question carefully to clarify your understanding and ascertain the facts of the situation – the cause of his problem. When you are both on an even keel again you can assertively negotiate a way forward.

Remember that if all else fails, you don't have to be a human punching bag. If the other person refuses to calm down or becomes abusive, you can assertively say something like 'This is getting us nowhere; I'll talk to you about this tomorrow' or 'I won't be talked to in this way' and then leave the situation.

THE STAYER

This is the person who talks on and on and seems totally disinclined to leave your home or your office. It is very tempting to use manipulative behaviour – to look pointedly at your watch, drum your fingers with impatience or yawn, hoping that she will get the hint, realize she's outstayed her welcome and leave. If your cues are picked up and acted upon, this could leave your visitor feeling slighted or guilty about their behaviour. It could knock their confidence. It is far more likely that they won't be that sensitive, so neither will they pick up your non-verbal message, willing them to go!

So what do you do? You can wait for a suitable pause in their monologue and say something like, 'It's good that you called in today because we've been able to catch up on old times, but I've got to prepare for my next meeting now...' and here body language can help in an assertive way. Get to your feet, offer a hand if it's a business associate, or walk past them to the door, leaving them in no doubt that as far as you're concerned, the conversation is at an end and you wish them to leave.

My doctor is good at this. He is prepared to listen and engage in a certain amount of social as well as professional chat, but you know when your consultation has ended when he pushes back his chair and, by subtle gesture, invites you to stand as he does. He then goes to, and opens, the door for you. This, combined with his manner, facial expression and caring attitude, leaves you feeling understood and cossetted – and he's kept to his timetable!

THE RABBIT

Barry has a problem. You are quite prepared to listen and help him find a solution, but can he get to the point? No, he can't. You have to hear every detail of every aspect of his life history and try to sift through this morass to get to the gist of his predicament.

Here you need good questioning skills so that you can interrupt in a constructive way to establish facts. You will need to reflect back for clarification, summarize occasionally, and ask further questions to help keep him on track.

Example

Barry: It's about where I work.

You: Where you work?

Barry: Well not *where* I work, but who I work with really. You know I'm on the same shift as Mike and Joe – they've been mates for ages, go everywhere together – I think they belong to the same sports club, you know that rugby club on the Gleathorpe Road, by the park....

You: So you've got a problem with working with Mike and Joe?

Barry: Well not a problem as such; it's just that I feel awkward with them sometimes. It's probably because of the way I was brought up, but I don't really like the way they talk to me. I'm no prude, but....

You: What is it about the way they talk that you don't like?

Barry: Well, it's difficult to put into words. Innuendo, my Mum calls it – snide remarks, like. I remember once she had the same problem with a woman at work. Mrs Hampshire I think she was called. She implied that my Mum....

You: Can you give me an example of what Mike and Joe say that you find offensive?

... and so on, keeping Barry on track, establishing facts, not being judgemental, not putting words into his mouth or offering opinions.

YOUR BOSS

I'm not suggesting for a moment that your boss is a problem person! He or she is probably extremely helpful and supportive. However, for most of us it is far easier to be assertive with peers and subordinates than to communicate assertively upwards – with professionals like doctors or solicitors or with bosses, directors or chief executives. This is especially true if the news you want to convey is constructive criticism, or information they would rather not hear – like asking for a rise or promotion.

Reticence is probably because of the power bosses wield by nature of their status. They can give or withhold, and generally have an impact on your future. Whereas most of the rules of good practice described in this book hold true when talking with your boss, obviously there are some things you wouldn't dare try!

I would suggest you periodically polish your self-esteem and practise self-affirmation so that when the occasion arises that you need to assert yourself with your boss, you are confident of your value to him or her and to the company, and of your right – as a useful member of the wider team – to have opinions about your environment and the work you do.

EXERCISE

This is similar to the exercise you did in Chapter 3, only there you were asked to list things you didn't like about yourself and work on those. That was far easier than what you will now be asked to do – to list your professional skills, your other talents and your personal qualities. Most people can think of plenty of negative attributes, but are coy about acknowledging their worth. However, it's amazing how gifted and wonderful you are when you stop and think about it!

List below at least 10 of your professional skills – things like office procedures you have mastered, technical skills, keyboard skills, foreign languages spoken and so on. (Think back to school and college days and also to previous jobs you've had.)

1	6
2	7
3	8
4	9
5	10

Next, list talents you have – perhaps innate talents such as being musical (break this down into what instruments you can play, whether you can sing, can read or write music). List other talents, such as do-it-yourself and what that involves, cooking, acting – whatever you enjoy and do well.

1	6
2	7
3	8
4	9
5	10

Finally, think of at least 10 positive qualities you possess – things like sense of humour, tolerance, flexibility, articulacy. There. You've got four already!

I am:

1	6
2	7
3	8
4	9
5	10

COMMENTS

Armed with this self-affirming information you should have the confidence to approach your boss about anything, knowing what an asset you are to any organization.

It is well to remember all your assertiveness skills when communicating with your boss. For example, when you enter his or her room stand tall with head up and look alert, don't slouch and present an apologetic appearance. Maintain good eye contact. Prepare well beforehand and be clear and concise in what you say. Use 'we' and 'us' to show you are part of a team. Maintain a pleasant and approachable demeanour. Know when to leave – your boss's time is probably precious. Always thank your boss for his or her support, and offer praise when appropriate. It can often be lonely at the top and bosses seldom get enough recognition and praise.

Demonstrate assertive behaviour at all times so that your boss can see that you are promotion potential. As an assertive professional you will be able to:

- speak up for yourself while respecting the views of others;
- calmly defend your position when necessary;
- make your ideas known and understood;
- influence without manipulating;
- say 'No' when appropriate, for yourself and others in your team;
- be effective in supervising others.

THE CRITIC

There's not one of us who can honestly say we enjoy being criticized, and it will take a lot of self-development and assertiveness training for your initial reaction not to be defensive or aggressive. It's human nature to protect our initial feeling of hurt pride or whatever by denying, justifying, rationalizing or counter-attacking.

There are many types of criticism from positive, constructive feedback to destructive verbal attacks. The first step is to recognize the criticism for what it is and then honestly decide whether or not there is any truth in it. From this you can decide how you want to handle the criticism: agree, partially agree, or disagree. Remember that it is the content of the criticism which has to be addressed, not how it is phrased or what you think is implied by your critic.

Criticism can be justified, unjustified or a mixture of the two. It can be delivered in an assertive or aggressive manner and the degrees of aggression can range from subtle to blatant. It is easy to recognize a destructive put-down when language, tone and body language all reflect overt aggression, but often it is only after the event that we feel somehow uneasy about an interaction and think, 'Wait a minute... when she said *that* she was *really* implying... what a cheek!' It is important to recognize put-downs for what they are, and deal with them spontaneously and assertively, as they happen.

Let's look at some examples. In each case A is the criticism, B is a reactive, non-assertive response and C an assertive response to the criticism.

Constructive feedback given in an assertive way

A 'I feel that by using the word "consequence" the client will perceive this as a threat.'

B (Defensive) 'Well how could he? It's obvious from the context what I mean!'

C 'Yes, I see what you mean; what would be a better way of phrasing it?'

Feedback given in an aggressive way

(The point is still a valid one, but opinions are stated as facts and criticism is of the person not the behaviour.)

A 'Don't use words like "consequence". The client will feel threatened if you send the letter out like that!'

B (Counter-attacking) 'I was adapting a letter *you* wrote; *you* used the word consequence twice in your letter to Mr Smythe!'

C (Fogging* and self-affirmation) 'You're probably right; I could have phrased that better. However, I feel you are making an assumption about the general tone of the letter. I'm satisfied with it.'

*For an explanation of fogging, please see below.

Criticism with which you totally disagree

A 'You look so scruffy with your shirt hanging out beneath your waistcoat.'

B (Aggression) 'Mind your own business. I'll dress as I please!'

C (Assertive contradiction and self-affirmation) 'I disagree. I think I dress fashionably.'

Note the difference between 'I disagree' as stated above, and 'you're wrong'. What effect would each statement have on you if you were on the receiving end of this communication? Assertiveness is about choosing appropriate terminology for each situation.

Fogging is a technique for coping with criticism described in detail in one of the classic books on assertiveness, *When I say no, I feel guilty* by Manuel J Smith (1975) Bantam Books. Half this book is devoted to sample dialogues, and although some are, perhaps, a little extreme in the light of recent thinking on assertiveness, they will give you a good feel for various assertiveness techniques described in the book. Stated simply, fogging means not denying the criticism levelled at you but agreeing, in principle, with any true statements or probable truths. It goes something like this.

Example

Tom: You made a real mess of that interview!

Harry: You may be right, I could have handled it better.

Tom: You gave the candidate far too much scope on that question of eligibility.

Harry: You've got a point; I could have tightened up on my questioning.

Tom: And why did you tell him all about the Naywell project?

Harry: I did go on about that, didn't I?

With fogging, you are not necessarily agreeing with the criticism, just acknowledging that the other person *may* have a point. You offer no resistance, so the other person has nothing to argue against. If you can become comfortable with fogging, you can lose the anxiety associated with receiving criticism. You know that you can cope with any criticism levelled at you without rising to the bait, getting ruffled, defensive or aggressive.

You can learn a lot about how your behaviour is perceived by actually inviting criticism. *Negative Enquiry* can help you find out exactly what it is about your attitude, performance or communication that has hurt, angered or affronted the other person. Negative Enquiry entails taking the initiative – asking questions to clarify, to elicit facts about your behaviour, to give more detail from which you can learn, or to enquire what else you do which might bother the other person.

Example

Ann: ... so you're annoyed that I overruled you on this occasion. Have there been other times when you've been unhappy with my decisions?

Bev: Well, yes, now you come to mention it. I feel that you undermined me when you told Mary to go to lunch. She's on my team; it's up to me to schedule lunchbreaks.

Ann: I can see why you feel annoyed; that shouldn't have happened. Is there anything else I do that interferes with your role as supervisor?

Bev: You could improve the way you delegate sometimes.

Ann: I don't understand. What is it about the way I delegate that can be improved?

... and so on. This example showed the manager requesting constructive feedback from one of her supervisors. It is also a technique which you, as a manager, could initiate with your boss to help you improve your performance. In other words, you can use Negative Enquiry up, down and across communication channels within the workplace.

If you are in control of your emotions, have a high self-esteem and are confident in your assertive role, you will be able to use Negative Enquiry to good effect to improve relationships in your personal life and at work. You can learn a lot about yourself if you actively encourage your critic to give you *constructive* feedback.

EXERCISE

There will be no comments offered on this exercise because how you respond depends on whether you can relate to the situations presented, how you feel you would react, ie whether you would be comfortable fogging or would feel the need to disagree totally or in part with the criticism. Remember to include statements of self-affirmation where appropriate.

Your boss: You are not pulling your weight.

You: _____

_____

_____

Your co-worker: You're too lenient with your staff.

You: _____

_____

_____

Your partner: You never do anything I want.

You: _____

_____

_____

KEY POINTS

- Apply the learning points from Chapter 2 – tension control and coping strategies, and Chapter 3 – positive thinking.

- Respect the other person's rights while not neglecting your own.

- Send the appropriate message by your choice of words, tone of voice, strength of delivery, and non-verbal signals.

TRICKY SITUATIONS

This chapter examines situations where you have to initiate what may be difficult interactions – such as giving criticism. It also touches on other areas where assertiveness skills are important to managers, such as attending and chairing meetings, and giving presentations, although the scope of this book does not allow an in-depth discussion of these roles.

GIVING CRITICISM

First, consider why you are criticizing the other person. Is it to get an annoyance off your chest; to 'have a go' at them to make you feel temporarily better, or is it to be constructive; to work together towards a change of behaviour or attitude which will benefit you both? Of course, an assertive person will always work to the latter set of criteria.

Giving criticism can be as stressful as receiving it – often more so – and the same preparation is required. Relax, think positively, and remember the needs and feelings of the other person. Use all your assertiveness skills and you will be fine. You may not be flavour of the month for a while, but far better for all concerned assertively to state your criticism. You may not be liked for it, but ultimately you will be respected – even thanked – for helping someone to improve performance, behaviour or attitude.

Let's go through the stages of giving negative feedback, step by step.

1 *Choose the time and the place carefully.* Usually it is best to offer the feedback immediately, so that the other person knows exactly to what you are referring and doesn't have to dredge his memory for the occasion in question. However, if other people are present, make sure you go somewhere quiet and private for the communication. Ensure that you have enough time to talk things through. Don't call him into your office five minutes before his allocated lunch break, for example. His attention will be on his hunger and the injustice of being criticized in his leisure time.

2 *Take care about the environment.* Are you both standing or sitting? Are you sending out non-verbal messages appropriate to the situation?

3 *Do you want to 'soften the blow' or does the criticism demand straight talking?* If the former, can you preface your communication with something like 'I appreciate that you've got a lot on your mind at present; however...'. Either this, or first remark on something good about the other person's work record or attitude, eg, 'I'm very pleased with the way you relate to the clients. However, I feel that you are having trouble with the paperwork – am I right?' Make sure that positive prefaces to criticism are truthful, not invented 'spoonfuls of sugar to help the medicine go down'.

4 *Use 'I' statements:* remember that it is you who want some sort of change from the other person, not the other way around.

'You' (blaming) messages label the other person in a negative way, eg, 'You need to brush up on your paperwork.' 'I' (rational) messages show that you take responsibility for requiring a change of behaviour, eg, 'I would like you to take more care with your paperwork.'

5 *Specify exactly what the person has done which bothers you.* Don't generalize. Talk about facts not opinions. Comment on behaviour, not personality.

6 *Don't be afraid to express your own emotions* if this helps give the other person an idea of the force of your feeling on the subject. This could range from, 'I'm embarrassed at having to talk to you about this' to 'I was furious when …'.

7 *Use silences.* After delivering your initial critical statement, which of course should be honest, clear and concise, allow the other person to respond. They may well require thinking time. Don't be afraid of an ensuing silence or be tempted to fill it by asking another question which will just confuse the issue and dilute the force of your original critical statement.

8 *Be persistent*, using Broken Record (see pages 100–05) if necessary. Explain what you want in the way of alternative behaviour. If appropriate, explain the positive aspects of change and/or the consequences of not agreeing to your request.

9 *Try always to end on a positive note.* Once you are sure that you have been heard and understood, and any agreements to change have been agreed, say something like 'I'm really glad that we both understand each other. Now tell me about that contract with Hustings & Co – I hear it's going well.'

COMPLIMENTS

We are often quick to criticize, but slow to praise. We are soon told when we make a gaffe, but doing well is mostly taken for granted. So acknowledge efficient work; thank people who take time to listen; praise initiative; recognize extra effort to do well or to please. Don't take for granted the meal that arrives at the table, on time, every evening, or the fact that the tyres on your car are always miraculously at full pressure without you having to check them, thanks to a thoughtful partner. Don't ignore subordinates who deliver your mail, wait at table, keep the car parking area neat and tidy.

Praise and thanks go a long way. If you ever need to criticize, your comments are likely to be more palatable if you are known to be fair with your positive and negative observations.

Some people find it difficult to compliment others on their appearance or behaviour. This seems to be especially true with people of opposite gender when meaning or intention might be misinterpreted. This doesn't alter the fact that most people are pleased to know that effort taken over personal presentation has been noted and approved, so practise giving *genuine* compliments in a non-threatening way.

If you receive a compliment, acknowledge it gratefully as a 'gift' from the other person, eg, 'Thank you – it was a Christmas present from my son. I like it too.'

ASKING FOR A RISE, PROMOTION OR CAREER MOVE

In Chapter 12 we looked briefly at assertively communicating with your boss. If you have done your preparation well by building a good rapport and by evaluating and believing in your own worth, the task of asking for an improvement in status or salary should be a lot easier. You will need to plan your meeting and rehearse your approach. Make an appointment, letting your boss know that you need his or her undivided attention to discuss something important to you. Depending on your relationship, this could be a formal meeting, or a talk over lunch in the local hostelry. Leave it at that – just make the arrangements. Don't begin to discuss the content of your proposed meeting then, or you may well 'shoot your bolt'.

You will need to practise all of your assertiveness skills – present yourself well, maintain eye contact, and show by your demeanour that you are confident and worthy of consideration. You will need to use language that your boss will relate to in a tone and pitch to match his. You will need to allow him to respond and listen well to what he has to say. Above all, you will need to sing your own praises – and this doesn't come easily to many of us. You must demonstrate why you deserve an increase in salary or promotion, giving examples of the work you have done and where you have 'gone the extra mile' for the organization. If you show by your choice of words, tone of voice and body language that you are serious and that this is important to you, you increase your chances of success dramatically.

If you get immediate agreement, great, but don't be down-hearted if your boss stalls. He may well need time to consider your request or discuss it with his superiors. However, you will need to be persistent and arrange a further meeting, by which time you should have some more points in your favour up your sleeve. The bottom line is, if you are worthy of advancement within the company and this is not recognized by management, you might be forced to look for more suitable employment elsewhere, and replacing you would be a costly business. You don't threaten this of course. Your boss will be well aware of the situation.

If you don't succeed in getting what you want on this occasion, use the opportunity to ask your boss what you need to do – what extra skills or experience you need to acquire – before you can be considered for promotion or a rise. Ask when your situation can be reviewed and get your boss to commit to a date. Remember that your boss may be restricted in what he can offer, but at the very least you are showing your determination to continue to improve your performance and to climb the corporate ladder. Remember to leave the meeting as assertively as you began it. Don't show disappointment, but thank your boss for his time with a smile on your face. Walk tall and confidently from the room.

It may be that you are not being as ambitious as this, but merely want a sideways move to improve your promotion chances in the future. The same rules apply. Prepare well and explain what you need and why you need it, using succinct language to which your boss can relate.

BEING INTERVIEWED

If two people are being interviewed for a job and both have exactly the same skills and experience, but one is self-effacing and the other is assertive, who is more likely to impress the interview panel? Doesn't it make sense to hone up on your assertiveness skills? If you can appear calm and confident, air your views adroitly and 'sell' yourself, you are far more likely to impress than someone who undervalues and understates his or her abilities.

Plan ahead. Consider the exercise you did in Chapter 12. You have innate talents and qualities, and over the years you have acquired many professional skills. Look at the talents you listed and break down the skills you require to accomplish the tasks involved. This will, if nothing else, be a huge confidence boost. Consider the likely and possible questions you may be asked and always answer by selling your strengths. For example, an interviewer may well ask you why they should give you the job. The question may be phrased differently, but something of the sort is usually asked at interview. You respond by saying something like, 'I feel that with my background in ... my experience with ... and my skills in ... I could help your company accomplish ...'.

When the time of the interview arrives, remember to dress appropriately and present yourself well. Walk into the room with an air of confidence and greet the panel with a smile. Shake hands *only if instigated by the interviewer(s)*, otherwise sit in the seat offered, adjusting yourself so that you are comfortable, upright and alert.

Remember to maintain positive body language in the way you sit, use your hands and so on. Control nervous mannerisms; resist the temptation to appear too laid back or over-confident.

When introductions are made, listen carefully for the names of people you don't know. Names are important to people, and if you remember and use them in conversation, their self-esteem is boosted and you are more likely to make a favourable and lasting impression. In a formal interview situation, even if you know one of the panel as Sally from marketing, give her the courtesy of her title and surname unless you are invited to do otherwise. Similarly, if someone previously unknown to you introduces himself as Marcus King, use his title and surname during the interview.

Make eye contact with each panel member, irrespective of who actually asks the question. They are asking on behalf of the whole panel, so include everyone in your response.

Be brief and specific in your answering, giving just sufficient detail to answer the question fully, and to do yourself justice. If necessary, ask if the panel would like more information on that point before proceeding.

If a panel member asks a discriminatory question which you would prefer not to answer (such as asking a woman what provision she would make should her children become ill – men aren't usually asked similar questions) say something like, 'I don't understand; could you explain the relevance of the question please'.

If a panel member is poor at interviewing and asks closed questions, help them out by offering more information than a 'Yes' or 'No'. In fact, this is an ideal opportunity to take some initiative in the interview and ensure that you say what you need the panel to hear.

Don't leave the interview without giving all the information you need to further your cause. If you can't fit this in to the questions asked by the panel, use the opportunity at the end of the interview when the panel asks, 'Is there anything you'd like to ask us?' to say something like, 'Yes, but before I do, there's something I would like to return to briefly …'.

If it looks as if you are to be dismissed without one of the inter-viewing panel telling you what the next stage is likely to be, and if you really want the job, you could say something like 'By the way, Mrs Smith, I would have to serve one month's notice, but could begin work with you immediately after that'. This might seem pushy, yet it can't hurt to show that you are keen.

PRESENTATIONS

It is not within the remit of this book to discuss the design and structure of presentations, but it is useful to look at delivery. Unless you are expert at writing in the same tone and manner as you speak, reading from written notes will make you appear formal and stilted. Be yourself; use vocabulary and style which you would use in normal, informal conversation. The audience want to be reassured that you are like them and that you understand them.

We speak in short phrases and sentences, using language which comes naturally. If you write down your thoughts and ideas, you will try to fit accurate vocabulary into grammatical sentences – as if you were writing an essay to be marked with points out of ten. I've tried to make this book as chatty and conversational as possible, but nevertheless have been careful, for example, not to split infinitives, although the resulting sentence may sound phoney if spoken aloud.

Rehearse your presentation well; have notes beside you for confidence by all means, but wherever possible, talk to your audi-ence in as natural a way as possible.

Dress appropriately for the occasion, but in something you find comfortable and which gives you confidence. How you look – how you feel about yourself – will affect the non-verbal messages you give out.

Know your audience and remember to match vocabulary to their level of knowledge and experience.

Overcome nerves or stage fright by using a relaxation technique. Accept that everyone gets nervous, and a certain amount of adrenalin rush will make for a better presentation. Tell yourself that, whatever happens, you can handle it.

Deliver your presentation with energy. Enthuse. Vary the pace and method of delivery to maintain interest. (Sparingly) sprinkle your talk with analogies and anecdotes; they will bring the presentation alive.

It's easy to find one or two people in the room with whom you feel in tune, and then make eye contact with them alone. I know it's reassuring to feel you've got supportive people out there, but share your attention with the whole audience. Make eye contact with as many of the group as you can.

Involve your audience by asking questions: hypothetical questions; ones to which you expect an answer; ones which you can pose, then answer yourself. This helps keep the talk lively, holds the audience's attention, and makes everyone feel included.

End your presentation on a strong note, then ask for questions from the floor. Here we return to the subject of the previous chapter – dealing with problem people – because some of the questions might be tricky. You can prepare for some through prior knowledge of the subject matter of your presentation, and of your audience. If you know your subject matter through and through, you will be able to answer questions of clarification; if the matter was contentious, you will be prepared for disagreement.

This won't stop you feeling slightly apprehensive, wondering just what you've let yourself in for! It's important, especially if feeling tense, to listen carefully to what is being said, rather than what is implied, so hear the speaker out before jumping in with a response. Be brief, succinct and to the point with your answers; don't begin a second presentation.

If necessary, buy yourself thinking time, and clarify the question by reflecting back, eg, 'That's an important issue; let me be sure that I've got it right. You feel that...?'

Don't get caught up in an interaction with just one member of your audience. Cut the dialogue with something like, 'It's obvious that we've both got a lot more to say on this subject; perhaps we can continue this at coffee?'

If a question floors you – you honestly don't know the answer – say so. Tell the questioner that you will find out and get back to her (and do it!) or suggest you send her some reading matter on the subject which she might find helpful.

If a member of the audience goes on and on without actually putting a question, you could say something like, 'Forgive me for interrupting, but because of time constraints I'm going to have to ask you to tighten up your question'.

If a member of the audience is overtly hostile, treat him as you would any angry person. Immediately acknowledge the hostility, 'I can see that you feel very strongly about this' or 'I see you're really concerned about this concept' which, in effect, gives him permission for his hostile feelings. Let him hold forth until the anger has begun to die down; then you can begin to discuss the issue rationally and on a factual level.

Remember, above all, you are in control. It's your presentation; it's your information; you control the pace; you can change the direction of the discussion. Whatever happens, you can handle it.

FACE TO FACE MEETINGS

Meetings, either on a one-to-one basis or with a group, can take up a large part of any manager's day. Good communication skills are important – influencing, persuading, listening, counselling – as is the ability to nurture relationships and goodwill within the workforce, with suppliers, customers and clients. This all calls for assertiveness. The non-assertive manager may let opportunities pass; the need to be liked may override the need to be effective; concern for the feelings of his team may cloud his judgement about what is ultimately best for them and for the organization.

The aggressive manager may get instant, short-term results but at the expense of long-term loyalty and commitment from his team.

Let's look first at your role as a participant at a meeting. Unless you have been allocated a seat, choose somewhere close to the Chair. To a degree this is a status thing, rather like sitting above or below the salt in medieval times. Anyone 'worth his salt' would be seated above the condiment, near to the host. Also, the main thrust of the conversation usually takes place near the Chair. The further away you are, the less likely are you to contribute fully to discussions. Another aspect is that if you are unsure of your ground, or don't wish to speak on a particular item, you are still seen to be 'in the thick of it'. Participating in an active listening capacity is far easier than if you were at the end of the table, on the periphery of the action.

In terms of positioning, remember that head-on orientation can be confrontational. This can make a subtle difference to the outcome of debates. It is preferable to 'line up' with known allies rather than be sitting across the table from them. Remember, too, that group dynamics can do strange things to people. Individuals behave differently 'in packs' than they do alone.

Listening is more of a problem at meetings than in one-to-one interactions. This is because everyone wishing to add to the discussion is mentally rehearsing their own contribution and looking for a suitable point to interrupt and have their say. Listening to the person presently holding the floor is therefore not as effective as it might be. You will need consciously to practise active listening if you are to get the most from meetings.

You will also need to practise assertively putting across your point of view, clearly, succinctly and with a force suited to the occasion. If you are supplying information, give facts not opinions. If you are disagreeing with the previous speaker, respect and acknowledge her views, though different from yours, before making your contribution. Avoid remarks like 'That's a ridiculous idea' which is a personal put-down; instead say something like 'I'm concerned about that proposal because ...'. Always try to offer an alternative rather than merely shooting someone else's idea down in flames.

If you are attending an informal meeting – in other words, you don't have to address your comments through the Chair – and you need to interrupt an aggressive contributor, be calm and wait for an opportunity to interrupt his or her flow. Use effective body language techniques to make it clear to everyone that you want to contribute at this point and, if necessary, use his name to get his attention – something like 'Peter, there's something I'd like to add at this point'. Match his volume and tone of voice until you 'have the floor'. Pick up from what Peter was saying to acknowledge that you have been listening to, and have understood, his views: 'I think I understand what you are saying – you feel that... but I feel we might look at this another way.' If Peter's aggression is in full flight, you may have to interrupt in a similar way several times, always using his name and demonstrating 'Broken Record' – rephrasing your comments until he has calmed down and will let you speak. Usually, assertive persistence will win out.

There are many skills to chairing a meeting which are outside the remit of this book. What we should briefly look at is the people aspect of successfully chairing a meeting. This will involve leading, guiding, questioning, summarizing and sometimes mediating skills. You have to accommodate the needs of the group, and of individuals within the group. For example, it is important to start the meeting on time in fairness to punctual members. Acknowledge latecomers, but don't recap for their benefit. They will soon learn that punctuality is an expected courtesy to the group.

It is the role of the Chair to ensure that everyone wishing to contribute, does so. This poses at least two problems: how to bring in the naturally retiring and quiet member, and how to control the talkative one!

There are several reasons why people are silent at meetings. Fear of exposure is not the least of these. To have one's lack of knowledge or experience publicly exposed can be a daunting prospect. Individuals may be shy. They might have views on the topic, but are not yet secure enough to express them in a group situation. They can be encouraged by being asked, by name, whether they have an opinion about a point just raised or, better still, how a proposed suggestion might affect the work of their department or whether an idea would work in their section. This gives something tangible on which to comment and is, perhaps, less threatening than having to voice a personal opinion. When a reluctant member does speak up, be sure to show interest (this doesn't have to be the same as agreement) to encourage future contributions.

If the members of the meeting are of different levels of seniority, more junior members may be reluctant to air their views in front of senior staff. Where you can, make it possible for them to give information or express their opinions to the group *before* senior members speak. A certain amount of stage management is important here. As with shy or reluctant speakers, ensure that junior staff contributions are welcomed and encouraged.

If someone goes on at length, use the good chairing technique of picking up an idea or phrase and offering it to another member of the group for comment, eg, '"The bottom line", David, do you see this as the bottom line?' The only snag with this is that you've got to know your members and be sure that David won't be thrown by being asked to contribute off the cuff in this way. If in doubt, it's best to ask 'Does everyone see this as the bottom line?' and hope that someone will pick up the gauntlet.

If a member is straying from the point, help him save face by saying something like, 'That's an interesting point…' but continue with '… but not really relevant to this debate, so we'll make a note to discuss it on another occasion'.

Body language can often help stem the flow of the garrulous speaker, not by impatiently drumming your fingers or by other aggressive gestures, but by fixed eye contact with a rapid nodding of the head to indicate that you have got their point and now want to move on. Swiftly move your eyes to someone else in the room, away from the talkative member, before posing a question demanding an answer, hopefully from one of the chosen few with whom you've renewed eye contact.

Be prepared to interrupt if two members lock horns in argument, if there is a personality clash or if splinter groups begin private conversations. A change of direction in the proceedings at this point is a good idea. Ask a factual question; get the whole group back on target and concentrated on the job in hand. This may need to be preceded by a ploy to gain attention. Usually, a loud, but relaxed and firm voice is all that's needed. Stay in assertive mode; don't become aggressive or bossy. Remind members of the goals of the meeting, of the issue under discussion and, if necessary, of time constraints.

Practise people watching. If someone is showing by their body language that they are in disagreement with, angered by or hostile to the flow of the debate, say it as you see it: 'Janet, I see you are bothered by this proposition.' Janet then has the option to put her point of view. If there is hostility, better to get it out in the open and deal with it right away.

Close on a positive note; summarize achievements, and remember to thank members for their time and contributions to the meeting.

EXERCISE

The following lines of dialogue show poor assertiveness skills. What is wrong? What would be a better approach?

Giving criticism

1 'What do you mean, I'm always late?'

Compliments

2 'Your holiday did you good – you look really great.'

'You must be joking. I've been back to work a week and feel shattered.'

Interviews

3 'Why should we offer you the position?'

'I don't know; there are probably others better suited – but I'll give it my best shot.'

Presentations

4 'You're obviously upset by my ideas on grumlet production, but what exactly *is* your question?'

Meetings

5 'Peter, you talk a lot, but have nothing to say. Either make your point or let someone else get a word in!'

COMMENTS

1 *Giving criticism.* The critic has obviously made the cardinal mistake of making a 'you' blaming accusation. He or she has also used a generalization, 'always', when no doubt the problem is a lack of punctuality, albeit on a fairly frequent basis. Nobody is always anything. If you're offering negative feedback, remember it's you who want the change, not the other person, so take responsibility for initiating the interaction by using 'I' statements.

   The person receiving the feedback should, of course, have countered with something like, 'Yes, I'm 15 minutes late today; but generally I think I'm quite punctual'.

2 *Compliments.* A compliment is a gift. If the receiver throws the gift back, it's tantamount to a rejection of the giver, and will be perceived as a slight. Be gracious in your acceptance. Say something like, 'Thanks, I feel better with a sun tan'.

3 *Interviews.* Being interviewed is not an occasion for self-effacement. Take every opportunity assertively to sell your skills, talents and attributes to the interviewing panel. This doesn't mean arrogance

or boasting, but a composed account of why you are the best person to meet the needs of the organization.

4 *Presentations.* The questioner may be incensed and taking a long time to get to the point, but don't imply that he is to blame for your incomprehension. Take the onus on yourself. Say something like, 'I can see that you're concerned about the changes I'm proposing. I want to answer you as fully as possible, so can I just check – you're worried about…?'

5 *Meetings.* The other members of the group probably realize that Peter's a bit of an idiot without you pointing it out to them! Whenever you need to interrupt someone – cut them off to allow others the opportunity to speak – help them save face by identifying something they have said and acknowledging its worth or interest before moving on to one of the tactics suggested in the text above.

KEY POINTS

- In potentially stressful situations, appear calm and confident in what you say, how you say it, and how you behave.
- When giving criticism relax, think positively and remember the needs and feelings of the other person.
- Be constructive, explaining clearly what the problem is and what is needed to be done about it.
- Talk about facts, not opinions; comment on behaviour, not personality.
- Use techniques described in earlier chapters to ensure communication is constructive and will ultimately benefit both parties.
- When receiving criticism, stay positive and seek a constructive way forward.
- Receive compliments graciously.
- Spontanaity can be achieved by rehearsing and practising techniques until they become second nature.

EVOLVING TECHNOLOGIES

The pace of change has never been greater. Communication options are continually expanding. By the time you read these words, there will already have been innovative changes to the technologies we use; new ways of doing everyday things; updated and upgraded ways of communicating electronically. While important to the ways we communicate socially, in the world of work, virtual workplaces are here to stay and require, not necessarily different, but refined communication and assertiveness skills.

Few people are ambivalent to technology; most either embrace the opportunities afforded by it, or fear – even hate it. Of course, it is personal choice whether you use an iPhone or a BlackBerry; whether you tweet, post videos to YouTube, keep a daily blog or communicate with your friends on Facebook. However, in business, the worldwide pace of change, where new technologies appear out of nowhere, means you need to adapt your assertiveness skills to embrace a virtual world.

In the late nineteenth century, telephones were considered 'new technology' and people had to get to grips with two-way communication where the other person wasn't physically present. New skills had to be learned, which still apply today. An assertive, good communicator realizes that although the recipient of a phone call may be miles – even continents – away, speaking with a raised voice is not necessary – a lesson which many people speaking on their cell phones in public places, restaurants, railway carriages, etc, could learn! In fact, an overloud voice could be seen as aggressive.

Good, assertive telephone skills are still very important for one-to-one personal and business exchanges, and also for teleconferencing where several people contribute from different locations.

If you are making a business call to one other person by phone, remember the etiquette required.

- Before you phone, be absolutely clear in your own mind what it is you want from the call. 'Oh, I forgot to ask…' type follow-up calls don't give a good impression.

- If the call is likely to be difficult and requires all your assertiveness skills, it will help if you stand during the call. The recipient won't know, but something as simple as changing to an assertive, open stance will give you that extra confidence.

- Give every business call the respect you would give the most important professional face-to-face communication.

- Greet the person, using their name – 'Good Morning, Mr White', etc, then say who you are and what the call is about using clear, direct and concise language. Don't overuse the person's name – once or twice depending on the length of the communication – but always close the conversation by thanking the person, by name, for giving you their time and attention.

- Remember that a telephone call *always* interrupts something the other person is doing. Show respect for this; ask if it is convenient to speak with them at this time. If not, arrange a time for your call, and keep to it.

- Don't waffle; you will be seen as indecisive and non-assertive.

- During telephone conversations, silences can seem extremely long, but if you've said what you want to say, and it's the other person's turn to speak, don't be tempted to fill the silence.

- Remember that the other person hasn't the benefit of visual cues to help understand meaning; won't be able to pick up subtle nuances.

- Use humour wisely. Without the benefit of visual clues, your wit could be misconstrued.

- Let your facial expression match the content of the communication; if you smile when talking, the recipient will recognize this and should respond accordingly. Similarly, if you need to be firm, let your facial expression, tone and pace of delivery indicate the seriousness of the situation.

- Avoid jargon and technical language unless you are sure the other person is on the same wavelength.

- Close the conversation ensuring that both you and the other party are clear about what has been achieved, what happens next, by whom and when.

- Thank the recipient for giving you some of her/his time.

There is one other thing to remember. Consider the following scenario:

> You have phoned a business colleague about a matter that is urgent and really important to you. It is obvious, from the intermittent quality of the transmission, that he has his phone balanced under his chin. You can hear shuffling papers and the occasional rattle of the keyboard as he 'multi-tasks'.

If you've been on the receiving end of this sort of discourteous behaviour, you will know how annoyed/hurt/frustrated this makes you feel. It's implying you're not important enough to be given the other's full attention. A non-assertive person with low self esteem may well feel flustered, and communication will suffer accordingly. As an assertive person you will, of course, be able to explain the effect the other's behaviour is having on you (using 'I feel...' rather than 'You are...' statements). Ask questions to open up communication, giving the other person a chance to explain. The other lesson to be learned, of course, is to be extremely careful about your own phone skills. Never make a business call while eating or drinking for example – the other person will know. Show respect for the recipient of your call by giving her/him your full attention for the duration of the conversation.

If you receive a difficult telephone call for which you are not prepared, far better to question assertively to ascertain the reason for the call, but give yourself time to gather your thoughts by stating something like: 'I appreciate your frankness, and understand why you should feel that way. I will get back to you when I've established the reason for...' etc. State when you will return the call, and stick to it. Take a deep breath; decide how best to respond, showing respect for the other person's point of view, while not losing sight of your own need for similar respect.

SOCIAL NETWORKING

The humble telephone as invented by Alexander Graham Bell has morphed into a myriad of devices from the basic mobile phone – limited to voice calls, texts and perhaps voicemail – to iPhones and similar multifunctional, pocket-sized computers whose main purpose is still to make phone calls, but which can do so much more. While technology is bringing more people together, making the world an ever diminishing place, it can also make individuals feel isolated as socializing and face-to-face communication is needed less and less in the business world.

Arguably, technology has created a make-believe world where, via Facebook, MySpace and the like, individuals can be (or appear to be) anyone they want. On the plus side, if you are not naturally an assertive person, you can *act* as if you are. Soon this acting will become a reality for you. On the minus side, social networking sites can be accessed by anyone, including potential employers to determine suitability for jobs. For this reason – if for no other – you should be careful about what you divulge and how you present yourself to the other person(s). The rules of the Equal Opportunities Act of 2010 can be applied to any written communication so, for example, racist or homophobic comments – even if written in jest – are there potentially for ALL to see and the consequences could get you into real trouble. So, at all times be conscious of the impression you are making. Only disclose what you are happy for *anyone* to see, because once it's 'out there', it's 'out there' for good!

Whatever you divulge via technologies should keep to all the assertiveness rules.

- Use affirmative, assertive communication.
- Project a confident self image.
- Use positive language.
- Regardless of whether you agree with them, let the other person express themselves without interruption. Expect, and if necessary request, the same respect when it's your time to speak.
- Respect other people's basic rights.
- Only divulge what you are happy for others to know.

TEXTING

Because users want to send messages quickly and with the fewest possible keystrokes, an internet shorthand – almost a new language – is evolving. Teachers in schools are despairing that children will think that 'you' is spelt 'u' or 'empty' as 'MT'. Even the oldest of us will recognise ASAP as an acronym for 'as soon as possible', but the current principle of abbreviating almost any word or phrase can result in a message incomprehensible to anyone not conversant with 'textspeak'. Ironically, it may be quicker to send messages using 'textspeak', but it can take the recipient far longer to decipher the communication than it would if standard English were used! It should be obvious that written shorthand should be reserved for personal messaging between family and friends, and should never be used in a business content.

E-MAILS

One of the decisions an assertive person needs to make is what method of communication best to use in each different situation, and not to get too dependent on just one or two forms. E-mails are faceless, so may well be attractive to non-assertive people. However, they are a good way to keep in touch with friends.

In professional life, e-mails are the twenty-first century version of an office memo. They are useful for sending reports and transmitting information. The same message can be sent to countless people, in many various locations, with just a few keystrokes. However, it is just as important to choose the most appropriate method of communicating for your purpose, not just the easiest, non-assertive type. It is impossible to know how often the other person checks e-mails, so if the message is urgent, e-mails are not the best choice. Similarly, in difficult or sensitive situations, how can you be sure that what you are trying to say in text, accurately conveys meaning? If you use capital letters for emphasis, or 'smiley' emoticons to indicate humour, the recipient could interpret this as sarcasm. Without instant visual cues you can't be sure.

If you need to reach just one person, telephone conversation may be preferable to e-mail; you achieve instant two-way communication and exchange non verbal cues – tone of voice, speed of delivery, etc. Even a walk across the office to have a face-to-face chat – old fashioned though this seems – is often more appropriate than any electronic means of communication!

The business e-mail has its pros and cons. On the plus side:

- it is efficient and provides a better use of time than telephoning;
- you can compose the e-mail when convenient to you;
- you are able to reflect before committing yourself to the communication;
- you can revise the communication before sending;
- several people can receive identical instantaneous information at the press of a key;
- it provides a paper trail for referencing back.

On the minus side:

- once sent, the paper trail exists;
- when the recipient chooses to read e-mails is beyond your control;
- e-mails and other inter-intranet communications can now be used as evidence in legal matters and can be taken as formal representations from your company.

This last point means that your written assertiveness skills need to be exemplary. Poor or inappropriate e-mails can 'come back and bite you'. Written assertiveness skills follow similar lines to spoken ones. To avoid misunderstanding:

- make a good impression by writing direct, clear and professional e-mails;
- compose carefully worded, concise sentences;
- follow business etiquette;
- do not use abbreviations or jargon unless you're sure that *all* recipients of the e-mail fully understand;
- if the content requires it, state your needs politely and firmly;
- make every effort to let the recipient know that their views are 'listened' to;
- ask for feedback such as 'how does this plan sound to you?' This shows you are considering their needs and are prepared to 'listen' to their input;

- proof-read before sending; could your wording be more effective – how would you feel if you received this communication?

- use a spell check. Above all else, check that you've spelt the recipient's name correctly;

- remember that once you've pressed 'send' there is no going back!

Two final points: be selective with the cc key. It is often easier and quicker to send e-mails to all when not everyone in your 'address book' needs or in fact *should* see the e-mail, so be selective. The second point is to treat e-mails as you would 'snail mail'. E-mails are not less important just because they are a faster way to communicate.

VIRTUAL WORKPLACES

Employees, managers and the self-employed are governed increasingly by the growth of technologies. Virtual teams comprise co-workers whose primary interaction is through some combination of electronic communication systems – telephone, e-mail, Skype, video conferencing and so on. Theoretically, individuals may never meet each other, and group dynamics change as members leave or join the team. If you are a manager creating a team of home workers, or organizing a team which contains people working from different sites or offices, an adapted set of skills is required to handle issues such as feedback and giving constructive criticism in a virtual world, without the traditional cues of social interaction.

In terms of assertiveness, if you are working from home or from an office where the preferred method of communication does not involve video images, act as if you are face-to-face with the other person(s). You will find it more difficult to maintain a professional and assertive presence if you are still dressed in your nightwear, or your hair needs washing! Sounds silly, but even if you're not seen, dressing and acting confidently *as if* you're in a face-to-face interaction, assertive behaviour is far easier and will be reflected to others.

If you are a 'virtual worker', being assertive is almost a pre-requisite because you will need to be self-motivated, focused and confident, and behave in a consistently positive and constructive way so that you can contribute fully to team effectiveness.

If you are a virtual team leader, you will need to apply your basic assertiveness skills:

- recognize that workers could feel isolated; keep all 'in the loop';
- encourage the exchange of ideas without negative criticism;
- promote honest, constructive communication;
- ensure all fully understand proposals, decisions, etc;
- express appreciation for good ideas and completed tasks.

It is not necessarily a more difficult task to be responsible for a virtual team than it is to be a line manager where the team are present. It just needs confidence and the application of all the assertiveness skills shown in this book.

VIRTUAL MEETINGS

The easiest option is using telephones for a conference call. This requires a speaker phone if there is more than one team member at a location. This has all the benefits of simplicity and cost, but you won't be able to see others' faces and body language, or detect how they are referring to written material.

Another option is to meet via personal computer. For this there needs to be a camera, microphone and speaker at each location. With this form of meeting, you have the benefit of being able to hear and also see each team member when it is their turn to speak. The disadvantage is possible image quality and natural delays between inputs – and of course, the other person will be able to assess you – not only by your appearance and manner – but by the state of your working environment which will be displayed on screen, so keep your desk space and workplace uncluttered and organized.

INSTANT MESSAGING

This involves using a chat room via your personal computer. You will need excellent keyboard skills to keep up with conversations, and an established etiquette and ground rules to ensure all contribute equally to meetings using this format. If you are organizing this type of meeting, it is a good idea to ask each person involved to identify themselves by a short 'nickname', their initials or by using a different colour and/or font for easy identification.

VIDEO CONFERENCING

There are many reasons why video conferencing is a more cost effective way for teams to use their time and be able to interact with other teams from anywhere in the world, providing the technology is in place. Assertiveness skills need to be modified to adapt to this virtual world. At the time of writing, some systems still suffer from screen wobble or break-up of image, and international conference calls can have an off-putting delay – you speak and there is a time lag before the other person responds. This unnatural break in the flow of conversation needs confident, assertive communication by all concerned.

If you are new to two-way, electronic communication, it would be wise to practise your assertiveness skills in a non-threatening environment. Ask a friend to record you, and be self-critical when you watch your image played back. Do you need to curb mannerisms and habits which could be distracting for others, such as clicking a pen, or fiddling with your hair? Everyone uses their hands to give emphasis to conversation, but do you overdo this to the extent that the other person is watching this rather than paying full attention to what you're saying? Can you maintain good eye contact when you are communicating with a camera or screen image?

When attending a virtual meeting, remember that even when you are not speaking, you will be 'on camera' to the other team. Here are some tips.

- Behave as you would in a face-to-face meeting. Just because you are not the one speaking, don't show boredom, get distracted, check your text messages, e-mails and so on. The other team will be able to see you!

- Do all you can to help your own confidence. Think about your appearance and wear clothes that are comfortable and smart. Best to keep to solid colour clothing because stripes and patterns seem more distracting on camera.

- Remember posture, and present yourself throughout as an assertive, confident person.

- In face-to-face communication, a head on stance can be seen as confrontational. However, in video conferencing, you are a two dimensional face on a screen facing another two dimensional face on a screen, so it's even more important to compensate by presenting positive body image, an assured manner and confident facial expressions. Don't forget to smile where appropriate.

- Even if you are not naturally assertive, *act* as if you are. You will convince others – and eventually yourself.

- When it's your turn to contribute, don't bend forward towards the microphone. Video conferencing equipment should pick up your voice from your natural sitting position, and leaning forward will affect your breathing and therefore distort your speech. You will look unprofessional and 'new' to electronic communication – not the assertive image you want to project.

- Always stay in sight of, and within the frame of the camera, otherwise the other person will feel as if they are talking to an inanimate chair and a disembodied voice.

- Eye contact is as important with video as with face-to-face communication, so don't keep your eyes lowered or on your paperwork. If you need to refer to notes, keep flicking your eyes back to the camera or screen to keep that close contact with the other person.

- The microphone is not selective. It will pick up splinter group whisperings. It can also pick up muttered comments better not heard, and which could prove disruptive.

- It will also pick up the sound of papers being shuffled, so keep notes, reports and so on away from the microphone.

If you are a manager who needs to set up a meeting, but decides that a face-to-face gathering is too costly in terms of travel, or that it's too difficult to get all participants to agree a date and time, a virtual meeting is the obvious answer. It is not in the remit of this book to list all the logistical do's and don'ts, but great care needs to be taken to establish ground rules such as not interrupting and being respectful of each other. Video conferencing requires adapted assertiveness skills. For example, you may need to speak a little louder than you would in a face-to-face situation; speak slightly slower and enunciate clearly. This may not come naturally to you or to members of your team, so you should practise to ensure that tone and extra volume don't convey aggression. At the meeting you should:

- introduce any new members – their name, role and function at the meeting;

- make clear who on your team is going to lead on each agenda item and ensure they keep to an agreed time limit;

- ensure that people take turns speaking and that everyone is included in the discussion;

- give the other person time to finish what they have to say, but if you need to move on to another person or a different topic, use techniques discussed elsewhere, such as little nods to show you've heard and understood but wish to interject;

- ensure that the meeting keeps to the main points;
- intervene appropriately where necessary to ensure everyone is understood, and understands. Check for meaning and rephrase unclear communication;
- remember that, without being able to see the finer points of body language, you may not be sure that communication has been received correctly or that others are listening; nevertheless, continue confidently; use summarizing techniques to keep the meeting on track and the participants aware of progress and decisions.

All of this needs confidence, self assurance and good assertiveness skills as discussed elsewhere in the book.

EXERCISE

You are an assertive person, communicating with family, friends, work colleagues, bosses and clients. Which method of communication would be most appropriate in the following situations?

1 You are in a one-to-one meeting with a client. Your partner texts you, asking if you would like to eat out tonight.

2 You have just received additional information regarding a work project, and your team – who are at different locations – need to know about this before your next face-to-face scheduled meeting.

3 You are in the middle of writing a report, and need to confirm a detail quickly with someone else in your office building.

4 You hear that a colleague is absent because of the sudden death of a close relative.

5 You are in the middle of a video conference for which you are responsible. There is a technical glitch and vision is lost. How would you continue?

COMMENTS

1 Technology is not more important than the live human being with whom you are currently communicating. Never cut someone off mid-sentence to attend to something which may or may not be more pressing. Only when a natural pause occurs, *and if the course of the conversation allows it*, ask if you might just check the text for importance. You should always give the person you are with your full attention and respect. A personal text such as the one described could be answered just by a simple 'yes' or 'can't do', but even transmitting something as quick and easy as that should be done when your original conversation has been completed.

N.B. It is not easy to remain in assertive, positive listening mode, with good eye contact, appropriate non-verbal behaviour and so on, when distractions occur. Practice is necessary to ensure you convey the message that the other person's views are important to you. Technology can wait.

2 E-mails are possibly the best and quickest way to convey the same information to several people at different locations. They also allow reflection and revision before sending.

3 Here a telephone call is more appropriate as only one other person is involved. If the person is close enough geographically, it might be a healthier option to walk to their desk where you have the benefit of visual and non visual cues.

One of the disadvantages of technologies is the isolation some people feel when all they are dealing with are letters, e-mails, chat room conferences, 'virtual' working colleagues. The personal touch shouldn't be ignored; in fact should be encouraged where at all practical.

4 Depending on how close you are to the bereaved colleague, a personal visit, a sympathy card or a hand-written letter by 'snail-mail' are the only appropriate responses. This is certainly not an occasion for any kind of typed or electronic communication.

5 Stay where you are during the interference as often the situation will rectify itself quickly and you can resume. If you leave your chair/the room and then are suddenly back online, it will not look good to the other parties if they are left looking at vacated chairs and an empty room. Apologize for the interference and any inconvenience, and move on. If the breakdown is more permanent, however, you should always have a back-up plan such as being ready to switch to a telephone conference. Throughout you will stay professional and unruffled, of course, using all your assertiveness skills to keep everyone informed and impressed by how you handled a difficult situation.

KEY POINTS

- Communicating electronically, where the other person(s) is not physically present, requires well honed assertiveness skills.
- Whatever you divulge via technologies is potentially accessible to anyone.
- Texting is appropriate for short messages which do not need the immediate response afforded by a telephone call. Never use 'textspeak' shorthand in a business text.

- E-mails are useful for transmitting information, globally, to any given number of people.

- Managing virtual workplaces requires an adapted set of assertiveness skills – for giving constructive criticism, for example – where there are no traditional cues of social interaction.

- Video conferencing requires modified meetings skills to match the virtual world in which we now live.

CONCLUSION

So, we come to the end of this grounding in assertiveness. Unfortunately, in the same way as you will not become slimmer and trimmer merely by watching a fitness workout DVD, neither will you become assertive just by reading words on the written page! You need to be actively involved in modifying your behaviour patterns to become more assertive, and thus more effective in social and business interactions – and you have to go out there and practise. Start with something small; be assertive over an issue that does not matter too much whether you succeed or fail. Practise your skills on someone you are unlikely to meet again, and if you make a mistake, forgive yourself, decide what you've learned from the interaction, and try again.

In choosing to be assertive you are not giving yourself control over your life. Whether or not you get what you ask for or achieve your needs, you know you have power over any situation, over your own feelings, stress levels and self-image.

Any form of self-development will affect existing relationships. Hopefully, everyone around you will be supportive, but remember to respect their feelings and the fact that they may need time to grow with you. If someone remarks, 'You wouldn't have said that a few months ago' you can assertively reply, 'You're probably right, I wouldn't. I'm pleased with the way I handled that. I like the new, assertive me!'

Creating Success series

The above titles are available from all good bookshops.
For further information on these and other Kogan Page titles,
   or to order online, visit the Kogan Page website at
   www.koganpage.com